Software

TIME
LIFE ®

This volume is one of a series that examines
various aspects of computer technology and the
role computers play in modern life.

COVER
The transformation of a random assortment of
colors into an orderly spectrum symbolizes
the governing role of software *(arrow)* in the
processing of information by a computer.

UNDERSTANDING COMPUTERS

Software

BY THE EDITORS OF TIME-LIFE BOOKS
TIME-LIFE BOOKS, ALEXANDRIA, VIRGINIA

Contents

The Invisible Instructor

Dwarfed by its huge booster rockets, the space shuttle *Columbia* stood poised on the launching pad at Cape Canaveral, Florida, early in the morning of April 10, 1981. Inside the cockpit, astronauts Robert Crippen and John Young lay strapped in their seats, ready to be lofted into orbit around the earth. It was a heady moment: For the first time in more than five years, Americans were about to venture into space. And for the first time ever, astronauts would seek to return to earth in a winged, controllable craft—one that could be used again and again on future missions. The weather was calm and clear. With 20 minutes left in the countdown, all seemed to be going according to schedule.

Suddenly, warning lights flashed on the computers at Mission Control in Houston: The shuttle's backup flight-system computer had detected errors in the linkage between Mission Control's computers and the shuttle, the so-called uplink that lets Mission Control take over shuttle operations from the crew if necessary. Technicians quickly discovered that the error messages were being caused by a timing discrepancy: Computer processes that were supposed to be synchronized were out of phase by 40 milliseconds.

The problem conceivably could have been cleared up by simply starting the programs over. But with the shuttle fully fueled, this option was deemed unsafe. In any case, until the nature of the timing problem could be determined, Mission Control would not allow the launch to go forward.

As Crippen and Young climbed dejectedly from the cockpit, analysts set about studying the flaw. They found that the phase-shift problem had its roots in changes that had been made over several years to the shuttle's highly complex system of software—the programs, or lists of instructions, that tell a computer what to do and when to do it. But they also found that the potential for mistiming introduced by these changes would occur only once in 67 launches—and then only during the initial process of getting the shuttle's computer programs running. Analysts assured the National Aeronautics and Space Administration (NASA) that a safe mission could be flown without any change to the software, and two days later *Columbia* blasted off without a hitch.

The software that runs the shuttle actually consists of eight separate programs, together containing approximately half a million separate instructions that monitor and regulate operations ranging from navigation and flight control to life-support systems. Such software ranks as a wonder of the modern world, a feat of construction that might be likened to the building of a pyramid—although in this case, the components are steps of logic rather than blocks of stone. Yet for all their

In a fanciful representation of the power of computer software, the program of instructions operating in a computer transforms an incoming rainbow into an intricate plaid fabric. Complex programs govern every computer application, from word processing to navigating through space.

intricacy, programs such as these differ only in degree from those that allow an accountant to do bookkeeping on a desktop computer or a child to play a game on a video arcade machine. Without programs, computers of any size are simply mazes of useless circuitry.

If the computer is thought of as a kind of musical instrument, then software is the musical score. The term "software" has been widely used since about 1960 to distinguish the instructions that run a computer from the physical components, or hardware, of the machine itself. In modern computing, these instructions are stored as magnetic signals on disks or on tapes similar to those used in tape recorders; a special part of the computer reads the signals into the machine, which turns them into coded pulses and stores them in its internal memory to direct subsequent activity. As its instructions are changed, the computer may shift from creating a graph to producing a standardized contract—or, with a larger machine, from manipulating an architect's blueprints to generating a weather map of the world.

Transforming a computer from one kind of tool into another was not always so easy. The behemoths that ushered in the computer age in the 1940s and

1950s required almost equal measures of mathematical ability and physical stamina to program. Mathematician Kathleen McNulty was one of the first programmers to work with ENIAC, a machine built at the University of Pennsylvania's Moore School of Electrical Engineering to calculate ballistic firing tables desperately needed by the United States Army during World War II. The tables gave artillery gunners the proper angle of elevation of their weapons needed to hit a target at a given distance, with an artillery shell of a given weight, and under varying conditions of air temperature and wind speed. Using an electromechanical desk calculator, a very skilled human took about three days to compute a single trajectory; the Army needed from 2,000 to 4,000 trajectories for each combination of weapon and shell.

Preparing ENIAC (for Electronic Numerical Integrator and Computer) to perform its operations was a maddening procedure. The machine was a monstrous conglomeration of vacuum tubes and plug-in cables, housed in 40 panels arranged in the shape of a horseshoe around the walls of a large room. "Somebody gave us a whole stack of blueprints," McNulty recalled years later. "These were the wiring diagrams for the panels, and they said, 'Here, figure out how the machine works and then figure out how to program it.'"

McNulty and the other ENIAC programmers—most of them women mathematicians—mastered the blueprints, determined how to rearrange hundreds of cables and devised settings for roughly 6,000 switches and dials. Getting the machine ready to compute one firing table required an average of two days of detailed manual labor.

Despite the frustrations inherent in the operation of ENIAC and its immediate postwar successors, it was through the use of these pioneering machines that most of the groundwork for programming was laid. Fundamental procedures invented in those early years have remained the basis for the elaborate systems of software that enable modern society to function.

FORERUNNERS OF THE COMPUTER ERA

Even as the war-spawned machines cast their shadows ahead into the future, their designs harked back to inspirations of an earlier age. ENIAC, for example, was modified so that data—though not programming instructions—could be entered with punched cards, a method of communicating with machinery that dates back to 19th Century French inventor Joseph Marie Jacquard. In 1804, Jacquard streamlined the weaving of elaborate silk brocades when he introduced a loom guided by stacks of punched cards, strung together to form a sort of tape. The workings of the shuttle were regulated by wooden pegs in a loom's "reader," which determined from the arrangement of holes which threads were to be raised or lowered to create the desired pattern. About 30 years later, the British mathematician Charles Babbage incorporated Jacquard's idea in the design of a remarkable device he called the Analytical Engine (page 10).

Much of what is known about Babbage's machine comes from the writings of the gifted amateur mathematician Augusta Ada Byron, the Countess of Lovelace. The daughter of the poet Lord Byron, Lovelace possessed an extraordinary intelligence. In 1843, she translated an article about the Analytical Engine written by an Italian mathematician, and she added her own copious notes on the machine's potential.

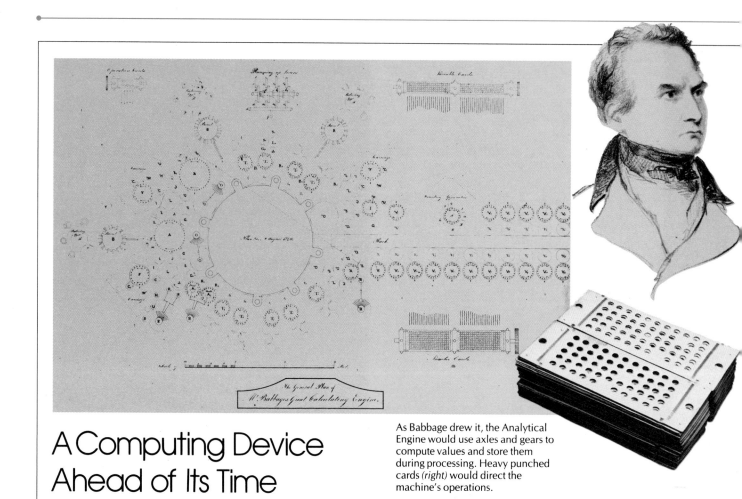

A Computing Device Ahead of Its Time

As Babbage drew it, the Analytical Engine would use axles and gears to compute values and store them during processing. Heavy punched cards *(right)* would direct the machine's operations.

In 1822, a British genius named Charles Babbage *(above, right)* embarked on a crusade that would absorb him for half a century. When he died in 1871, he left more than 400 square feet of meticulous drawings, many of them for the Analytical Engine *(above)*, a forerunner of today's programmable computers. His first effort was to build something called the Difference Engine, designed to produce complex mathematical tables accurately and automatically. After 12 years, beset by technical, financial and political setbacks, he abandoned the project and began work on the Analytical Engine, a more sophisticated machine that would be capable of performing a wide variety of tasks; for each job, instructions and values would be entered on punched cards. Babbage devoted the rest of his life to his inspiration, but the manufacturing precision it required was far beyond the technology of the period, and it was never completed.

As Babbage envisioned it, the Analytical Engine was intended to solve not just one type of calculating problem but a wide variety of them. In fact, Babbage had conceived and designed a general-purpose, programmable computer incorporating many of the features that characterize modern machines. Although he never succeeded in building this ambitious device, his detailed plans show, for example, that the Analytical Engine was to have a section called the store, for holding the numbers to be processed; this was the equivalent of a modern computer's memory. And punched cards — which could be changed according to the desires of the operator — would guide the machine's labors. Lovelace, one of the few of Babbage's contemporaries to grasp the significance of his achievement, wrote that a machine so versatile would have a value "almost incalculable in its possible ultimate results."

Nothing resembling the Analytical Engine would appear for nearly a century, but the notion of using punched cards in processing data was put to the test far sooner. Within 20 years of Babbage's death, the American inventor Herman Hollerith devised an electromechanical counting machine that used punched cards to tabulate the results of the 1890 United States census. (As it happened, Hollerith got the idea not from Babbage's work but probably from observing a railroad conductor punch tickets.) The tabulator was so successful that Hollerith established his own firm to meet the growing demand for his invention. Eventually the company became International Business Machines, or IBM, the corporation that made punched cards a standard computer programming medium.

A COMPUTER PIONEER IN GERMANY

Hollerith had shown that punched cards and electrical circuitry could work together to perform useful tasks, but his device was limited to tabulation, pure and simple; the punched cards could not direct more complicated computations. One of the first truly programmable computers was created by a German engineer named Konrad Zuse, who built a number of calculating machines and computers in the late 1930s and early 1940s to solve complex engineering equations.

Zuse's machines, which were controlled with perforated strips of discarded movie film (his ingenious answer to a wartime paper shortage), employed electromechanical relays of the sort then used in telephone switching circuits. Zuse was also one of the first computer engineers to build an operational machine (the Z3 in 1941) that used the two-digit binary number system instead of the more familiar decimal system. In the binary system, any decimal number can be encoded as a series of ones and zeros — a method somewhat confusing to the human eye but perfectly suited to the two-state, on-off operation of an electric circuit. Equally important to the development of modern computing, this two-state system is also easily adapted to encoding the true-false operations of symbolic logic, which makes a computer more than just an arithmetic machine.

Because of the war, Zuse's work was not known outside Germany for many years. As it happened, other scientists on both sides of the Atlantic were also pursuing the elusive goal of designing programmable machines. Several of them had arrived at conclusions similar to Zuse's about the efficiency of the binary number system and symbolic logic for electric computing, but the conversion from decimal to binary was not immediately universal.

While Zuse carried on with his labors in Germany, American scientists were working on two projects that would loom large in the history of programmable computers. At Harvard University, mathematician Howard Aiken and a team of IBM engineers were putting the finishing touches on the five-ton, $500,000 Mark I, a program-controlled calculator intended to solve naval ballistic problems. Like Zuse's machines, the Mark I used electromechanical elements and was governed by instructions encoded on punched paper tape. It could multiply two 23-digit decimal numbers in three seconds, and it was flexible enough to perform calculations for a variety of defense-related problems during the war. Although other machines soon surpassed it, the Mark I served at the Harvard Computation Laboratory until 1959. More important, perhaps, it provided a

One of the few people who understood Charles Babbage's Analytical Engine was the Countess of Lovelace, sometimes regarded as the first computer programmer. While theorizing steps the machine would follow to solve problems, she introduced several techniques that are still used today for directing program flow. She described, for example, instructions to repeat a series of steps until a given condition is obtained—an operation now known as a loop.

training ground for several computer pioneers who would later make notable contributions to the fledgling science.

The other American project was ENIAC, whose awkward programming requirements would be the bane of technicians like Kathleen McNulty. Designed by John W. Mauchly and his Moore School colleague J. Presper Eckert, ENIAC—like the Mark I—operated with decimal rather than binary numbers. But its use of vacuum tubes instead of electromechanical relays for computation made it a thousand times faster than the Harvard machine.

In building ENIAC, Mauchly and Eckert had made a technological leap of faith, for no machine had ever before used more than 2,000 vacuum tubes. ENIAC incorporated nearly nine times that number. The tubes' tendency to burn out was not a small problem: During one year of ENIAC's operation, about 19,000 tubes had to be replaced, more than 100 per cent of its total tube complement. Even so, ENIAC demonstrated that electronic computation was the way of the future.

The main advantage to electronic computers, as Mauchly and Eckert realized, lay in their potential for storing large quantities of information. The rotating shafts and cogged wheels of electromechanical computers were ill suited to the building of memory devices large enough to hold more than a pittance of data in the machine itself. With the advent of electronics, such internal memories were suddenly feasible.

But ENIAC itself was only a first step in that direction. Designed under the hurry-up pressure of wartime, ENIAC had only limited internal storage. Although it could execute complicated programs very quickly, its accumulators—the array of vacuum tubes designed to hold data for computation—could store a total of only 20 decimal numbers of 10 digits each. And although the contents of this internal memory could be changed quickly, changing instructions to the machine required the time-consuming wrangle with pluggable cables and banks of switches.

Two years before ENIAC went into operation in 1945, Mauchly and Eckert were already dreaming of a better machine, one capable of storing not only large quantities of data but the program's instructions as well. Their idea—a stored-program machine—changed the face of computing and paved the way for the development of modern programming languages. Mauchly and Eckert called the new design EDVAC, for Electronic Discrete Variable Automatic Computer. For internal memory they planned to employ devices called mercury delay lines. Used during the war to time radar signals, delay lines were tubes of mercury in which electronic pulses bounced back and forth to be retrieved at will. EDVAC also was designed to utilize binary rather than decimal numbers, thus simplifying the construction of its arithmetic units. As they worked on its design, their ideas were synthesized in a landmark paper written by the brilliant, Hungarian-born mathematician John von Neumann, then on loan from the Institute for Advanced Study at Princeton. Von Neumann, who had acted as a consultant on the ENIAC project, intended his 101-

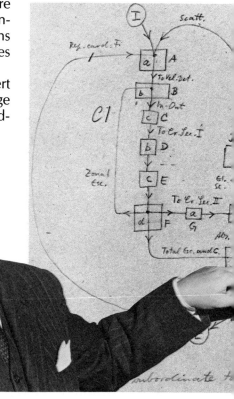

In this composite image, mathematician John von Neumann, who brilliantly synthesized the concept of storing a computer's instructions in its own internal memory, points to an early programming-flow diagram. Taken from one of his papers, the diagram simulates subatomic particle collisions.

page paper only as a rough draft, to be read, evaluated and revised by the EDVAC team. Instead, one member of the team, Herman Goldstine, sent the report—titled "First Draft of a Report on the EDVAC"—to more than 30 people in June of 1945, listing von Neumann as the only author. Certainly von Neumann's contributions to the report were significant, particularly with respect to the logical operation of the machine. Furthermore, his lustrous reputation gave the paper a range of influence it might not otherwise have had, thus ensuring continued support for the project. But it also led to a general belief that the stored-program computer was his invention.

The premature distribution of the EDVAC report caused years of bitterness and ultimately resulted in Mauchly and Eckert's losing their claim to patent rights. For a host of reasons, of which EDVAC was only a part, the pair left the Moore School at the end of March 1946, to form their own company. With the EDVAC team thus depleted, work on the computer ground to a halt.

Despite the controversy, the idea of machines with programs stored internally began to catch fire, particularly in England. One person who received a copy of the EDVAC report was J. R. Womersley, an official of Britain's National Physical Laboratory, who had been invited by the United States to visit the ENIAC and Harvard Mark I projects. Womersley returned to England with a copy of the EDVAC report, eager to organize a British project along the same lines.

The first scientist he recruited was Alan Turing, one of a group of researchers who had worked during the war on the highly secret British codebreaking machine called Colossus. Turing's contributions to computing had begun a decade earlier, when, at the age of 25, he wrote a paper titled "On Computable Numbers." The paper envisioned a hypothetical device consisting solely of an endless tape and a scanner that would read and act on symbols marked on the tape. The machine would be capable of solving any legitimate problem of mathematics or logic. Turing's purpose was not to invent a computer but to describe problems that are not legitimate—that is, are not logically possible to solve. However, his hypothetical machine foreshadowed certain characteristics of the modern computer. The endless tape, for example, can be seen as a kind of general-purpose internal memory.

With Turing's help, Colossus succeeded brilliantly at its mission—to crack the messages generated by the German code machine Enigma. Although it was designed to be a special-purpose logical computer, it was actually flexible enough to execute many different tasks. And because it was the first machine to use large quantities of vacuum tubes (it went into operation two years before ENIAC), Colossus also served to train a cadre of researchers in the new field of electronic computing—a corps that would give Britain a quick start in the race to build a stored-program computer. (Ironically, at about the time Colossus was being built, Konrad Zuse was trying to persuade the German government to fund a similar device, using vacuum tubes, specifically to decipher British secret codes. His petition was refused, on the ground that the war would be over before he could get the machine running.)

Assigned by Womersley to study von Neumann's report and develop a computer like EDVAC, Turing came up with a plan for a machine he named ACE, for Automatic Computing Engine. He even wrote some primitive programs, using an alphanumeric code. But the ACE project hit a succession of bureaucratic snags, and Turing left in frustration long before a small-scale version—called the Pilot ACE—was completed in 1950.

Turing's next stop was Manchester University, where a team headed by Max Newman was working on another computer project. Newman, one of Britain's foremost mathematicians, had helped originate the Colossus project and was certainly familiar with current developments in the field. Even before Turing joined the team, Newman's group had built a small working prototype of a fully electronic stored-program computer, called the Manchester Mark I.

MEMORY ON DISPLAY

For its internal memory the machine used electrostatic storage tubes—six cathode-ray tubes (CRTs) like those used for radar displays and for television monitors. The base of the tube held an electron gun that shot a beam of electrons at the inside surface of the tube to form charged phosphor spots. The beam pulsed on and off in response to instructions from the computer, producing spots that corresponded to the zeros and ones of the binary code. By regenerating the charge every $\frac{1}{30}$ second, the contents of the tube were maintained. An array of special electrodes placed close to the outside of the face of the tube enabled the computer to detect, or read, the location of every charged spot. And because the spots were also visible to a human viewer, one tube was set aside to give the Mark I's operators a visual display of the contents of any of the tubes.

At first the system had some difficulties. When the start switch was flipped on, "the spots on the display tube entered a mad dance," chief engineer F. C. Williams recalled. "In early trials it was a dance of death leading to no useful result, and what was even worse, without yielding any clue as to what was wrong." But on June 21, 1948, the Manchester Mark I ran the world's first stored program—a search for the highest factor of a number—and, to Williams' delight, "there, shining brightly in the expected place, was the expected answer."

Even as the Mark I blazed its shining trail, another group of Britons, at Cambridge University, was putting the finishing touches on a machine that would demonstrate the true capacity of stored-program machines. EDSAC, for Electronic Delay Storage Automatic Computer, was virtually a direct copy of Mauchly and Eckert's EDVAC: In the summer of 1946, Maurice Wilkes, director of the university's Computer Laboratory, had come to the United States to attend a series of lectures on the subject of stored-program machines given at the Moore School by Eckert, Mauchly and others.

As Mauchly and Eckert had proposed for EDVAC, the British machine's internal memory was built of mercury delay lines. They were slower and more expensive than CRTs but could hold more information—and were more reliable as well. EDSAC beat the luckless EDVAC by two years, becoming operational a year after the Manchester Mark I, in June of 1949.

With the introduction of machines equipped with internal memory and with circuitry designed to process data in binary form, computing was on the verge of realizing its great potential for versatility. But Alan Turing and others recognized that most programmers would have more than a little difficulty addressing their machines in look-alike strings of ones and zeros, the so-called machine code that is a computer's fundamental language. As a first attempt to ease the programmer's burden, Turing wrote a manual listing a kind of shorthand code for writing

Machine states	If scanner reads a blank	If scanner reads an X
STATE **1**	STOP	Erase; change to state 2; move left
STATE **2**	Write; change to state 3; move left	Remain in state 2; move left
STATE **3**	Write; change to state 4; move right	Remain in state 3; move left
STATE **4**	Change to state 5; move right	Remain in state 4; move right
STATE **5**	STOP	Erase; change to state 2; move left

The Logic of a Turing Machine

While studying at Cambridge University in 1936, British mathematician Alan Turing wrote a paper titled "On Computable Numbers." In it, he described a hypothetical device — subsequently known as a Turing machine — that presaged the programmable computer. Designed to perform logical operations, a Turing machine can read, write or erase symbols written in squares on an infinite strip of tape. At each step in a computation, the machine's next action is determined by matching against an instruction list whatever symbol the scanner is reading.

In this example, a Turing machine is set up to double positive whole numbers. Its instructions describe five states, with the machine required to perform different actions in each state. The machine begins in state 1 with the scanner positioned at the start of the data — here, the number 2, represented by two Xs in a row on the tape (top). When the machine stops after 16 separate steps, the tape contains twice as many Xs as before (bottom).

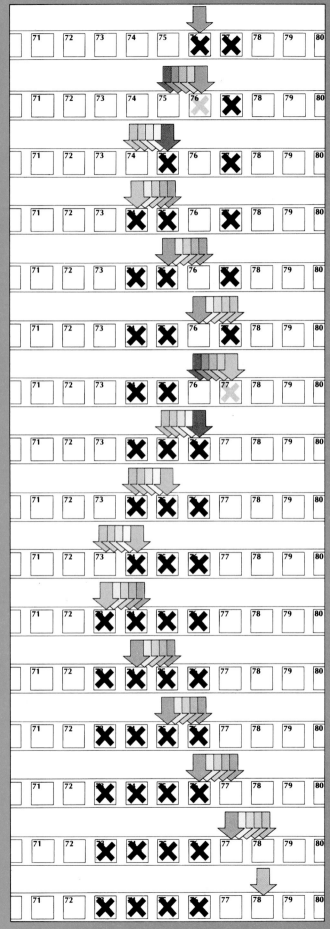

programs for the Manchester Mark I. The code used combinations of teleprinter keystrokes to represent long strings of binary digits. The letters *TC*, for example, corresponded to the zeros and ones that the computer understood to mean "add." The teleprinter produced a punched paper tape, which was fed into the computer; the Mark I then read the pattern of punched holes as the equivalent of ones and zeros and translated these into a string of high or low pulses.

CREATING UNDERSTANDABLE CODES

Using a teleprinter rather than setting switches was certainly a step in the right direction, but it did not go far enough. Alick Glennie, one of Turing's associates at Manchester, saw complicated programs as the major obstacle to the development of the machines and any widening of their use beyond the confines of research laboratories. "To make it easy," he wrote, "one must make coding comprehensible. Present notations have many disadvantages: all are incomprehensible to the novice, they are all different (one for each machine) and they are never easy to read. It is quite difficult to decipher coded programs even with notes, and even if you yourself made the program several months ago."

John Mauchly, among others, agreed. By this time, the company he and Eckert had formed was working on the design of two computers: a binary device called BINAC for Northrop Aircraft Corporation, and the Universal Automatic Computer, or UNIVAC I, for the U.S. Bureau of the Census. In 1949, Mauchly directed his programmers to devise a program that would enable the machine to accept algebraic equations as originally written. Although the result—dubbed Short-Order Code and also called Short Code—did not achieve that ambitious goal, it did allow the elements of an equation to be represented by a two-character code rather than by strings of binary numbers. An equation such as $A = B + C$ could be entered as *00 S0 03 S1 07 S2*, where *S0*, *S1* and *S2* stood for the variables *A, B, C;* and *03* and *07* stood for the operations of equality and addition (the *00* was the line number in the program). A programmer could then instruct the computer to assign the value *5*, say, to the variable *S0*, and the value *3* to the variable *S1;* the computer could then solve for the value of *S2*.

Mauchly's Short Code was a revelation to one of the company's harried programmers, a feisty, independent woman named Grace Murray Hopper. "I think this was the first thing that clued me to the fact that you could use some kind of code other than the actual machine code," she recalled nearly three decades later.

During World War II, Hopper had joined the WAVES (Women Accepted for Voluntary Emergency Service) and been assigned to the Bureau of Ordnance Computation Project at Harvard. There she became, in her words, "the third programmer on the world's first large-scale digital computer," the Harvard Mark I. "We were not programmers in those days," she remembered. "The word had not yet come over from England. We were 'coders.' " But Hopper and her coworkers, Robert Campbell and Richard Block, were laying the groundwork for programming methods that have held up surprisingly well.

Because its chief assignment was the computation of ballistics firing tables, the Harvard Mark I had some general mathematical operations wired into it. But Hopper and company found that the solving of a particular problem on

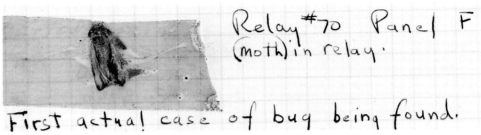

Relay #70 Panel F (moth) in relay.

First actual case of bug being found.

Grace Murray Hopper, a mathematician and pioneer programmer, developed considerable troubleshooting skills as a U.S. naval officer working with the Harvard Mark I and its successors in the 1940s. She found—and documented in the Mark II's log—the first real computer bug: a moth that was trapped in one of the thousands of electromechanical relays inside the machine, bringing work to a halt.

the machine usually required something more specific. So they coped as best they could. "We started writing subroutines," she remembered, referring to sets of instructions used repeatedly and designed to form part of larger segments, or routines, within a program. And when programmers needed a subroutine someone else had already written, they copied it out of that programmer's notebook. Although the word "subroutine" itself was coined later, one of the fundamental elements of modern programming was in operation as early as 1944.

The following year, Hopper and her colleagues christened an equally elementary—albeit less appreciated—aspect of computing. One hot and humid summer day, a mysterious malfunction caused the newly completed Harvard Mark II, an improved version of the Mark I, to be shut down. Upon investigating, the programmers found that an electrical switch was blocked by the remains of a moth that had somehow found its way into the computer's maze of circuitry. Ever attentive to detail, they extracted the dead moth with tweezers and taped it into the meticulous logbook that they kept on the Mark II's work for the United States Navy. The accompanying notation recorded the "first actual case of bug being found." As Hopper recalled later, "From then on, when the officer came in to ask if we were accomplishing anything, we told him we were 'debugging' the computer." The term stuck, and finding problems with a computer, particularly with its software, would forever after be known as debugging.

In 1949, Hopper joined the Eckert-Mauchly Computer Corporation to work on UNIVAC I. She stayed with the organization, through its acquisition by Remington Rand and its later merger with the Sperry Corporation to form Sperry Rand, until her retirement from the UNIVAC division in 1971. During this period in computer history, she worked tirelessly to promote the idea that programming should be done in higher-level languages—that is, in something as close to natural human language as possible.

"Those were precarious days," she said, recalling the time when Eckert and Mauchly's fledgling company was housed in an old factory in North Philadelphia. "We used to say that if UNIVAC I didn't work, we were going to throw it out one side of the factory—which was a junk yard—and we were going to jump out the other side, which was a cemetery."

Mauchly's Short Code, despite its undeniable advantages over programming in binary machine code, was not a panacea. Because it was sufficiently removed from the zeros and ones of machine language, it actually needed a silent partner—another program—to translate it into the computer's binary code. A program entered in Short Code had to be scanned and executed line by line by a translating program called an interpreter. Thus, every single operation in the program had to be spelled out fully whenever it was needed—even if it had been used several times before.

Then, in October 1951, Grace Hopper was given an assignment to build a set of standardized mathematical subroutines for UNIVAC I. In the course of this work, she noticed that—like the programmers on the Harvard Mark I—her colleagues were copying routines and subroutines from one program into another. "There were two things wrong with that technique," she said. One was that copying a subroutine into another program meant changing all the numbers, or addresses, that designated where the routines were to reside in memory; since these addresses were usually blocks of numbers in sequence, inserting them into another program meant adding onto a sequence already established—"and programmers are lousy adders," Hopper said.

They were also notoriously poor copyists. "It was amazing how many times a *4* would turn into a delta, which was our space symbol, or into an *A*—even *Bs* turned into *13s*," she said. "All sorts of things happened when programmers tried to copy subroutines. And there of course stood a gadget whose whole purpose was to copy things accurately and do addition."

A PROGRAMMING BOON

Out of this observation of human fallibility was born the A-0 compiler. The compiler was a program that was used to help in the writing of programs. Given an identifier, or call word, it instructed the computer to pull a particular subroutine out of a kind of library of subroutines stored on magnetic tape and read it into a portion of the machine's memory. The computer would extract a number of different subroutines and compile them accurately into a program; no *Bs* would turn into *13s*, no addresses would be added incorrectly. Delivered with the UNIVAC computers that went to market in the early 1950s, compilers made possible the automatic program—so named because the machine itself had taken over much of the tedious work of stringing together program instructions.

Rudimentary as it was, automatic programming was a godsend to the harried data processors who inherited these machines, for software was not available off the shelf. Once an organization acquired a computer, someone still had to write a program specifically designed to get the machine to keep track of the company's payroll or the nation's census data or whatever else the machine was supposed to do. As one programmer later remembered of this period, "the cost of programming was at least equal to that of the equipment."

Thanks in large part to Grace Hopper's indefatigable energies, compilers and similar programming aids helped secure commercial success for UNIVAC, which became the first computer to be manufactured and sold in significant quantities. In 1951, the first UNIVAC was delivered to the United States Bureau of the Census, with four other machines destined for the armed services and other agencies of the federal government. And in 1952, UNIVAC faced the nation on television, accurately predicting the landslide presidential victory of Dwight D. Eisenhower over Adlai E. Stevenson—but only after a team of programmers had invented the program that allowed UNIVAC to analyze precinct voting patterns.

Building on the performance of UNIVAC, other manufacturers jumped into the computer business, and it became apparent that a technological revolution had begun. The revolution was founded on two main elements—the motionless swiftness of electronics, and a language that was moving steadily toward the goal of human-like communication. The incalculable value of computing, foreseen more than a century before by Charles Babbage and the Countess of Lovelace, was well on the way to becoming a reality.

Putting Software in Control

Computing power even greater than that of the giant machines of the 1950s can now fit on a silicon sliver the size of a fingertip—an amazing feat of miniaturization that has put computers within the reach of almost everyone. Moreover, modern machines can perform tasks scarcely dreamed of when computers relied on vacuum tubes and punched cards.

The secret to this versatility lies in the software, or programs of instructions, that give a steel-and-silicon machine its myriad personalities. Unlike programs for the earliest models—which had to be physically wired into the machine by the tedious process of setting huge banks of switches and dials—the software that animates modern computer hardware is encoded on recording tape or metal or plastic disks and is available as soon as the machine is turned on.

Despite this vastly more convenient method of giving a computer its instructions, the fundamental nature of those instructions has changed very little. Every computer must break the job down into a series of logical operations and then perform these operations one after another.

Over the years, computer software has evolved into several main types of programs. At the center of most computer systems is a particular combination of programs called the operating system. Operating systems coordinate the computer's duties and manage the storage of programs and other information. The operating system tells the computer how to interpret instructions and data; how to allocate its hardware resources to perform a job and how to control peripheral devices such as a printer or a video screen. It also provides ways for human and computer to interact directly, organizing such activities as the movement and storage of programs and data files.

If the operating system is the stage manager of the computer show, application programs are the stars. These are the programs, such as word processors, games and spreadsheets, that make a computer so versatile.

The term "software" also includes programs called translators and utilities. Translators are used by programmers to help create applications software; they convert statements of so-called higher-level languages, which resemble human speech, into machine language, the zeros and ones that computers process as pulses of electricity. Utilities perform mundane but often required tasks such as sorting and merging files of data. These unobtrusive workhorses are used with even the most sophisticated application program to help it do its tricks.

From Input to Output: The Computing Process

Every computing job involves putting information into the computer, processing it in a specified way and issuing the results. The computer does the work with a complex system of components. Input devices such as keyboards or hand-maneuvered "mice" allow information and programs to be fed into the computer; temporary, or read-and-write, memory (often called RAM, for random-access memory) holds information and programs during processing; output devices display the consequences of the processing. External storage devices, such as disks or tapes, provide long-term electronic

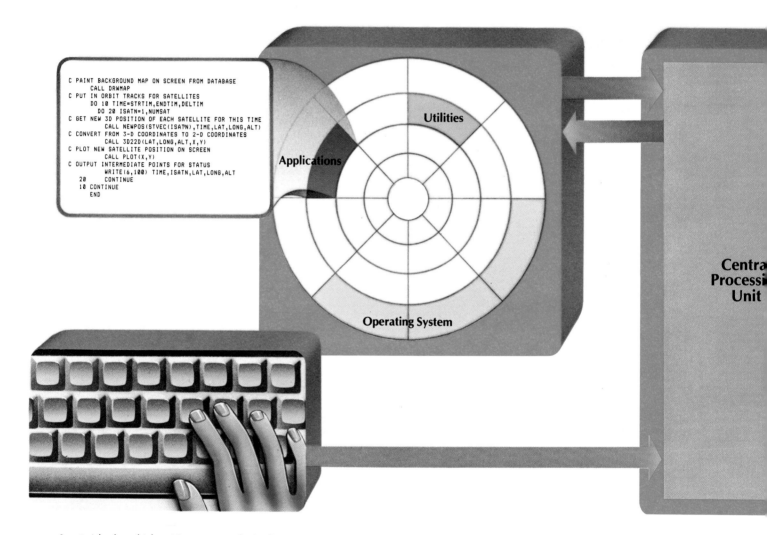

```
C PAINT BACKGROUND MAP ON SCREEN FROM DATABASE
    CALL DRWMAP
C PUT IN ORBIT TRACKS FOR SATELLITES
    DO 10 TIME=STRTIM,ENDTIM,DELTIM
    DO 20 ISATN=1,NUMSAT
C GET NEW 3D POSITION OF EACH SATELLITE FOR THIS TIME
    CALL NEWPOS(STVEC(ISATN),TIME,LAT,LONG,ALT)
C CONVERT FROM 3-D COORDINATES TO 2-D COORDINATES
    CALL 3D22D(LAT,LONG,ALT,X,Y)
C PLOT NEW SATELLITE POSITION ON SCREEN
    CALL PLOT(X,Y)
C OUTPUT INTERMEDIATE POINTS FOR STATUS
    WRITE(6,100) TIME,ISATN,LAT,LONG,ALT
 20    CONTINUE
 10 CONTINUE
    END
```

Utilities

Applications

Operating System

Central Processing Unit

Input. A keyboard *(above)* is a common device for communicating with the computer. The software controlling the machine identifies certain combinations of keystrokes as instructions to act on or as data to be processed. Simple programs can be entered by means of the keyboard, but longer or more complex programs are usually loaded into the computer's memory using a device such as a disk drive *(top)*, which transmits information stored on a disk to the machine. Disks are organized in concentric circles to hold different types of data and programs recorded as magnetic signals the computer can read. Part of a program to track satellites is shown here.

filing for programs and data. These devices combine input and output functions: The computer can copy information from a disk into temporary memory for processing, and copy the results of processing back onto the disk or tape.

At the heart of the computer's system of hardware is the central processing unit (CPU), which coordinates the movement of information and does the actual computing. The CPU is designed to recognize an instruction set—electronic codes that tell it to perform specific functions. All programs are made up of sequences of these codes; when a program is run, the CPU executes the instructions one at a time, at very high speed.

A few fundamental programs are permanently stored in the computer's read-only memory, or ROM. When the computer is turned on, the built-in programs give the CPU its initial instructions, telling it how to find the operating system on a disk or tape and copy it into temporary memory. The operating system then takes control of all the system hardware, and establishes a set of user commands and computer responses that allow the user to control the computer.

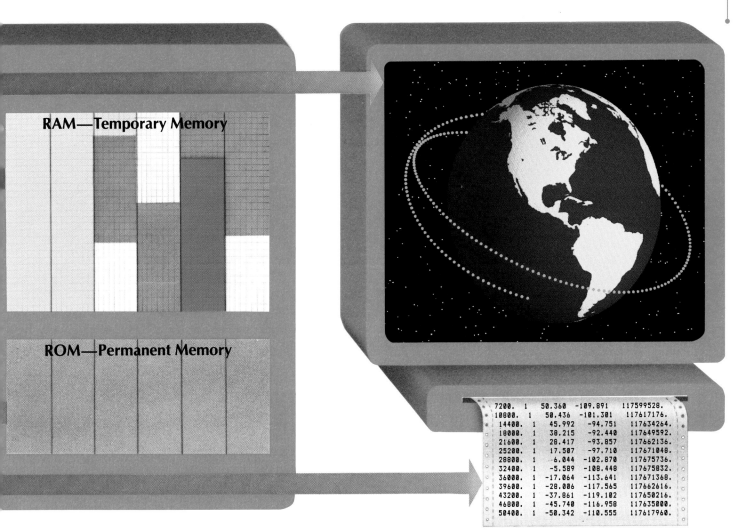

Processing. Within the CPU, a control processor directs the order of operations, while an arithmetic logic unit performs calculations and logical functions. When active in the computer, a program resides in temporary memory (RAM), so that the CPU can fetch instructions one at a time, in sequence. Programs permanently set in the circuits of read-only memory (ROM) provide orders for starting the computer and instructions for communicating with input and output devices. ROM may also hold a language such as BASIC for user programming or programs for applications such as word processing.

Output. A video display unit shows the graphic results of computation. Usually the computer displays input from the keyboard as well as its own responses. The screen changes rapidly as the program carries out its tasks, allowing rapid interaction between the user and the computer. A printer can produce a paper, or "hard," copy to record the results of a program *(above)*. Output may also take the form of an artificial voice or control impulses for a robot arm or a spacecraft.

Mapping Memory for Program Storage

Fast, accurate access to the programs that control the CPU and to the information being processed enables a typical computer to perform hundreds of thousands of operations each second. To make this access possible, programs and data are stored as a series of coded electronic pulses—representing the binary digits 1 or 0—in arrays of microelectronic cells in temporary memory, or RAM *(right)*. Each cell holds a single binary digit, or bit, and cells are grouped together in larger units called bytes *(below)*. Permanent memory, or ROM, whose contents cannot be erased or altered, is configured in a similar fashion.

Each byte of memory has a unique address. The CPU can read the contents of a particular byte of memory by sending an electronic signal to the appropriate address. The CPU can also transmit information to any address in temporary memory, where it replaces whatever is already stored there.

A program is usually held in memory in a block of bytes, with lists of instructions stored at sequential addresses. This simplifies control of the program flow, since the CPU does not have to be told after each step where to look for its next instruction; instead, it automatically calls the contents of the next memory address in the sequence, unless explicitly told to go elsewhere.

Temporary memory is also used to store information that is being processed. The program reads data, works on it and stores it back in memory, keeping track of all relevant addresses. Instructions in each program also tell the CPU what type of information is stored at each address.

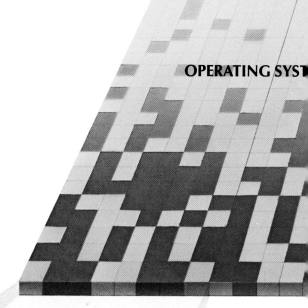

OPERATING SYST

A simple, versatile code
A computer's memory is made up of thousands of electronic switches, each capable of holding one of two states: on or off, corresponding to one bit of information, either 1 or 0. Groups of eight bits, called bytes, provide 256 (2^8) possible combinations of 1 and 0, which can represent a variety of symbols *(opposite)*, depending on the dictates of the software controlling the computer.

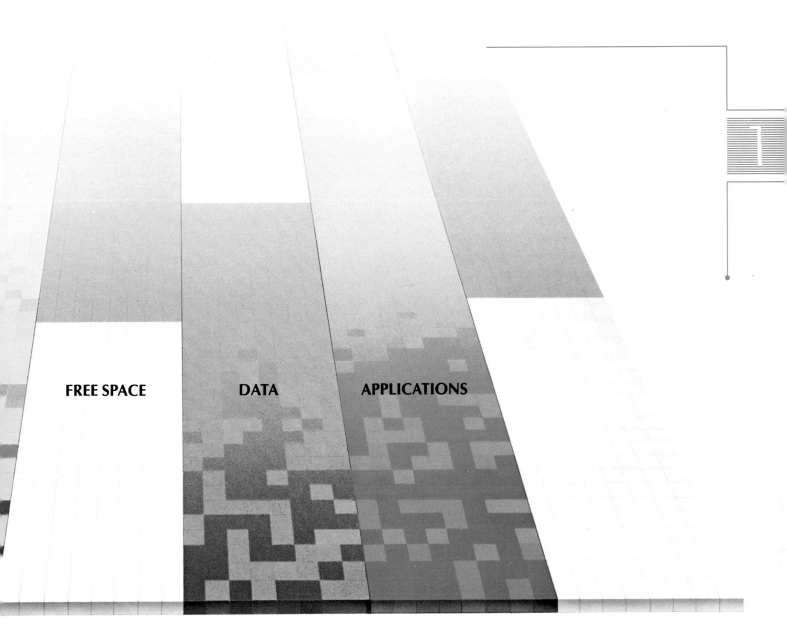

FREE SPACE   DATA   APPLICATIONS

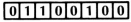

A character in a byte
A special code, the American Standard Code for Information Interchange, or ASCII, assigns a decimal number between 0 and 127 to letters of the alphabet, to digits 0 through 9 and to a set of punctuation symbols. Translated into binary digits for the computer (the letter *d* is shown here), the code numbers provide a standard format for exchanging data between computers.

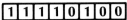

A command in a byte
The contents of a byte—or of a series of bytes—can also be interpreted as an instruction for the central processing unit, which tells the CPU to perform a certain job. Instruction codes are unique to each model of CPU; the one shown here would cause one kind of CPU to come to a complete halt.

A number in a byte
Numbers used as values for computation are not represented in ASCII but in different binary codes. In one system, a byte can encode any decimal integer between −127 and +127; more bytes are used for large numbers and fractions. Other coding schemes use a fixed number of bytes to approximate a value.

A symbol in a byte
One of the most powerful attributes of software is its ability to ascribe any meaning at all to a particular byte configuration. In addition to encoding letters, numbers and program instructions, bytes could be used by the software to encode such things as musical tones or shades of colors.

23

New Languages for Problem Solving

In the mid-1950s, as computer science took root on university campuses and at research institutions across the United States and Europe, programming entered a period of explosive progress. This burst of development did not sweep away all that had gone before; rather, it built on foundations already established: Compilers and interpreters remained essential to the programming of every computer, as did so-called assembly languages, which require an intimate knowledge of machine hardware. But while these fundamental programming tools went on performing their necessary functions, they gradually became invisible. A new kind of language, more fluid and sentence-oriented than assembly language, arrived to mediate between human programmers and their machines.

With the advent of the higher-level languages, programmers could devote more time to solving the problem at hand and less to worrying about the fine points of how the machine would go about doing the job. And with these languages also came the first steps toward programs that went beyond the confines of the research laboratory and the payroll office.

Two important figures in the developmental surge were Thomas Kurtz and John Kemeny, members of the mathematics department at Dartmouth College. Kurtz, who joined the Dartmouth faculty in 1956 after receiving his doctorate in statistics from Princeton, had first encountered computing at a summer session on numerical analysis at the University of California at Los Angeles in 1951. Kemeny, less than two years his senior and also the recipient of a doctorate from Princeton, had been in on the ground floor of computing. In 1945, while still a Princeton undergraduate, he went to Los Alamos, New Mexico, to work on the top-secret *Manhattan Project* to build the atomic bomb. His superior there was none other than John von Neumann, whose own ideas on computing had a lasting influence on the field.

Like von Neumann, Kemeny was a Hungarian immigrant with a genius for mathematics. He also had a knack for using logic to beat the system. In 1942, as a bewildered 16-year-old with very little English, Kemeny took a verbal aptitude test administered by his teachers at Washington Heights High School in Manhattan. "I had no vocabulary and could understand just a few words of each question," he recalled years later. "But it was a multiple-choice test and I understood enough to see there was a pattern to the answer key. I cracked the code and got one of the highest scores in New York City."

After the war, Kemeny served as a research assistant to Albert Einstein at Princeton's Institute for Advanced Study while finishing work on his doctorate. Unable to find a position teaching mathematics, his first love, he taught analytic philosophy for a while. Then, in 1953, he was hired to chair Dartmouth's mathematics department. He was just 27 years old.

When Kemeny and Kurtz began their association, Dartmouth, a small liberal arts school in Hanover, New Hampshire, did not even possess a computer. Yet within a decade, thanks to the efforts of the two colleagues, the college not only would boast an impressive computer center but would claim honors as the birthplace of BASIC, a programming language of great popularity and impact.

THE TRIALS OF BATCH PROCESSING

In those early days, however, Kemeny and Kurtz had to run their math programs on whatever computer they could find. The nearest one—a new IBM 704 with the then-phenomenal ability to store 8,192 thirty-six-bit words in its internal memory—was 135 miles away at the New England Regional Computer Center at the Massachusetts Institute of Technology in Cambridge. And even if Kemeny and Kurtz made the journey, they were still forced to keep their distance from the machine, owing to the cumbersome system known as batch processing. Because computers were so rare and so expensive, they were not made accessible to just anyone. Instead, programmers were required to keypunch their instructions for the computer on IBM cards and then hand the cards over to the designated operator at the computer center. This intermediary fed the cards into the machine in a large batch, often consisting of hundreds of separate programs, from scores of programmers.

Then the waiting began. Not until the computer had processed the entire batch of programs, which could take up to 24 hours, did it spew out printed responses. Even then, the response was often frustratingly incomplete: Something as minor as a missing parenthesis was enough to cause the machine to stop the program, and the print-out would thus contain only a cryptic error message. The programmer would then correct that line in the program and wait, sometimes until the next day, for the opportunity to slip the corrected program into the next batch of cards going into the computer. If there was another error, on another line, the process would begin again. Even very good programmers often took as long as two weeks to find and correct all the bugs in a single program. For Kurtz, whose task it usually was to carry programs to the MIT computer, it all boiled down to innumerable train rides to Boston.

As if batch processing were not enough of a burden, the earliest programming on the 704 had to be done in assembly language, just one step up from having to write everything in binary ones and zeros. Whenever a program misfired, the only way to discover the error was to read so-called memory dumps—long printed strings of cryptic numeric codes.

Kemeny and Kurtz cut their programming teeth on the 704, learning assembly language and reading endless memory dumps. Although Kemeny in particular had hopes of bringing computing to Dartmouth, he despaired of ever being able to teach the subject to his colleagues and students unless the process could be made considerably less daunting.

By the early 1960s, the two men had made progress of sorts. For one thing, Dartmouth had acquired a small computer of its own in June 1959—a Royal McBee LGP-30 with a memory about half the size of the 704's. Kurtz became head of Dartmouth's brand-new computer center, and over the next few years, the two professors and an assortment of their students experimented with creating simple languages to run on the LGP-30. One undergraduate with no computing experience devised a language and a compiler he named DART. The student's achievement confirmed something Kemeny and Kurtz had believed all along, namely that computing was well within the reach of undergraduates.

Eventually the time seemed right to go ahead with a plan they had been mulling over for years. It was a radical proposal, but the two men succeeded in winning the support of the college: Dartmouth would teach the rudiments of computing to all its students—science and non-science majors alike.

Such a goal was extraordinary enough, but Kemeny's intended method was even more remarkable. Unlike his counterparts on other campuses, who were content to teach computing through lectures, Kemeny wanted students to learn about computers by actually programming them. But first a couple of rather large hurdles had to be cleared. For one thing, even if Dartmouth students had to travel no farther than their own computer center, there was still just the one machine and the seemingly inescapable tedium and frustration of batch processing. Engineering and math majors might be compelled to put up with waiting hours or days for results, but English and history majors were sure to balk.

If the prospect of batch processing was not enough of a deterrent, the problem of teaching non-science students a programming language should have been. By this time a few higher-level languages had appeared. First among them, and the one then most widely used, was FORTRAN, developed in the late 1950s by a team of IBM programmers. Designed to express scientific and mathematical formulas, FORTRAN, for Formula Translator, was not easy even for engineers to master. For example, $DO 150 I = 1,10$ is the start of a programming loop that tells the computer to repeatedly perform the instructions immediately following that directive—up to and including the instruction numbered *150*, the first time with *I* equal to *1* and with *I* increasing by one each time until *I* equals *10*. If the programmer inadvertently typed a period instead of a comma between the *1* and the *10*, the statement would instead be interpreted as assigning the value *1.10* to a variable named *DO150I*. The statement would be valid—"legal," in programming jargon—but the program would not produce the desired results.

The Dartmouth duo refused to be intimidated by such obstacles. As a start, they began looking for an alternative to batch processing. They found it in an idea—first proposed at MIT in 1959—called time sharing.

Time sharing involved linking several keyboard terminals to one mainframe. (At the time, the word "mainframe" simply referred to a computer's central, or main, processor, which directs the machine's activities; in modern parlance it is often used to refer to a large, powerful computer as distinguished from desktop or other less powerful models.) Special programs enabled the mainframe to switch its attention from one terminal to another, doing a small part of each user's job in a specified period of time (a "time slice," usually measured in milliseconds). Because the mainframe could process information so rapidly, each programmer seemed to have the machine's undivided attention; in fact, of course, the programmers shared the computer's time. This was just what the Dartmouth system needed, Kemeny and Kurtz decided.

Next, they set out to create a programming language that their students could readily learn. The language they envisioned would consist of words from simple

English, including commands such as SAVE, RUN and LIST. Its syntax would be similar to FORTRAN's, but much easier to understand. For example, to get the computer to write a particular phrase, the programmer would merely type the instruction PRINT, followed by the phrase enclosed in quotation marks. Their new language was intended to be so undemanding, Kemeny said, "that students could use it after three hours of training."

AN ALL-PURPOSE DESIGN

Some of the ideas developed by Kemeny and Kurtz were new, such as the INPUT statement. Because students would be typing their programs in at a terminal rather than handing punched cards to a computer center operator, the language was specifically designed to be interactive—that is, to allow a programmer to modify a program as it was running by interrupting it to put in (or input, in computer jargon) new data or instructions. And unlike FORTRAN, which requires the programmer to distinguish between integers and so-called floating point numbers (numbers such as fractions, which the computer represents by, in effect, moving the decimal point), Kemeny and Kurtz's language called for numbers to be treated in just one way. Thus a student programmer need not remember that dividing the integer two by the integer three produces a number different in kind from either two or three. As Kurtz later put it, "Almost anything you typed for a number was legal."

The new language received a fitting name: Beginners All-Purpose Symbolic Instruction Code, or BASIC. And it was definitely intended to be all-purpose. With it, a sociology student could write a program to sort the results of a statistical survey, a French student could write a program that conjugated regular verbs and an engineering student could write a program to calculate the weight-bearing characteristics of different bridge materials.

In the summer of 1963, Kemeny began work on the compiler for a draft version of BASIC. That fall, two students began designing and coding the operating system for the machines the project would eventually use, a General Electric 225 and a Datanet-30, both acquired with grants from the National Science Foundation and a discount from GE. In February 1964, the equipment arrived on campus and the pace of development quickened.

Finally, on May 1, 1964, all these efforts came together. At 4 o'clock that morning, in a basement on the college campus, Kemeny and his colleagues sat at three teletype terminals and began tapping out programs. "We had done that many times before," Kemeny remembered later. "But that was the first time they worked. That was the simultaneous birth of BASIC and time sharing." By June, three terminals had increased to 11, and by fall, 20 of them were available.

Time sharing soon became the standard method of computing in large organizations such as universities, government agencies and corporations, albeit usually with languages other than BASIC. BASIC itself went on to become the grass-roots language of programming—a result of its almost universal adoption as the built-in language of the microcomputers that burst on the scene in the late 1970s. By the mid-1980s, several million American schoolchildren had learned BASIC. And around the world, more people were conversant in it than could speak the Scandinavian languages of Norwegian, Swedish and Danish combined.

Higher-level languages, sparse in the early 1960s, eventually came to number in the hundreds, if their various dialects are included. This has led to several attempts to create a universal tongue for programming. None have been entirely successful; in programming, it seems, tailoring produces the best fit. Of the dozen or so most widely used languages, each is intended for a particular kind of task. BASIC, for example, is still a common tongue for writing simple programs, especially on microcomputers. FORTRAN, with its precise numerical requirements, remains a programming classic—a kind of software Latin or Greek—most appropriate for scientific, mathematical and engineering applications. Another tongue, COBOL—for Common Business Oriented Language—was created in 1960 by a joint committee of computer manufacturers and users to serve as the main language for large-scale data processing in government and business. With COBOL, unlike most other languages, all data must be described separately from the instruction portion of the program, a convention that allows the same data description to be shared by different programs.

Other languages are even more specialized. For example, LOGO (from the Greek for "word") is widely used to teach schoolchildren to program. It allows the beginner to control the movement of an onscreen character called a turtle. By typing commands such as FORWARD 60, LEFT 45, FORWARD 75, the young programmer tells the computer to draw a straight line 60 units long, make a 45-degree counterclockwise turn and draw another line 75 units long.

Another important language is ALGOL, for Algorithmic Language, algorithms being the step-by-step procedures for solving a given problem. The first version, ALGOL 58, was devised during an eight-day meeting in the late spring of 1958. Computer scientists from the United States, including John Backus, one of the creators of FORTRAN, met in Zurich with their counterparts from the European computing community to hammer out what was intended to be a universal, machine-independent language of the same level as FORTRAN but without FORTRAN's close association with IBM and that company's machines. ALGOL 58 and its successor, ALGOL 60, met with mixed reviews. They never gained the wide acceptance ultimately accorded FORTRAN, but they were a significant influence on the development of many subsequent languages. One popular derivative of ALGOL-60, a language known simply as "C," has become the standard choice for programs requiring detailed control of computer hardware.

Two other languages created in an effort to improve on ALGOL are Pascal and Modula-2, both developed by computer scientist Niklaus Wirth of Switzerland. In Pascal, which Wirth produced in the late 1960s, the programmer must define all variables in a separate section at the beginning of the program. Because these definitions must be explicitly declared, Pascal programs are relatively free of errors and are easy for someone other than the programmer to understand and modify. This disciplined approach makes Pascal extremely well suited to novice programmers. Wirth's second language, Modula-2, preserves the logical organization of Pascal but allows software to be written in separate "modules," a practical feature that simplifies the construction of large programs.

Despite the proliferation of languages in which to write programs, software development has lagged far behind technical advances in the computers themselves. While hardware steadily increases in power and decreases in price, software has grown so expensive that it often accounts for more than 80 per cent of the total cost of a large new computer system. Indeed, engineers complain that software is typically the "gating item," the bottleneck that holds back new hardware and new applications.

Software has become a bottleneck largely because of its ever-increasing complexity. Many programs are so big that they defy comprehension even by computer scientists. In the mid-1980s, for example, the software that handled air-traffic control at 20 sites in the United States and one in the United Kingdom had more than 600,000 separate instructions to the computer. Of these instructions, no fewer than 39,203 were so-called conditional branches—points at which control of the program could flow in either of two directions. As a result, the number of possible paths through the program was astronomical, approximating the number 10 followed by 11,800 zeros. By the end of the decade, the program had nearly doubled in size, greatly multiplying the number of paths.

(In a conditional branch written in BASIC, the line might read *IF N ≥ 4 THEN 220*. This tells the computer to jump to the instruction on line 220 *IF* the variable *N* is greater than or equal to *4*; if *N* is less than *4*, however, the computer would automatically proceed to the next line in the program.)

But the complexity of software derives only in part from the intricacy of the problems to be solved. It is inherent in the very nature of the programming process, which demands great patience and precision in translating problems into terms the computer can grasp.

ABOLISHING AMBIGUITY

In programming, nothing can be left to chance. Actions a nonprogrammer might take for granted must be spelled out for the machine in excruciating detail. As one computer scientist has pointed out, "If a human can think about how to do something, it doesn't seem like a big problem. But a human uses marvelous abilities, like associative reasoning and pattern recognition."

Every projected action for a computer must be broken down into its most elementary components to produce the procedure known as an algorithm. In its simplest form, an algorithm is not unlike a recipe for baking a cake. But a computer programmer must specify component steps that the human mind tends to skip over. A cake recipe, for example, might call for three eggs—without specifying that the eggs must be fresh, not hard-boiled, and must be cracked open to use only the liquid insides.

When hundreds or thousands of instructions covering every contingency have to be spelled out for the computer, expense naturally rises and bugs creep in. These everyday-variety bugs are what the Dutch computer scientist Edsger W. Dijkstra has called "minor annoyances in great multitude." Dijkstra, a professor of computer science at the University of Texas, is one of the world's most influential theorists of programming and an outspoken critic of what he considers the malpractice of it. He has for years contended that most errors are preventable and stem largely from the sloppy manner in which programming has evolved as an intuitive, seat-of-the-pants art rather than as a rigorous science.

In a world where word processing is now the norm, Dijkstra's chosen method of disseminating his controversial views has been characteristically unconventional. From his home in Austin, he periodically issues a newsletter called *EWD* (from the initials of his name). He writes *EWD* in longhand, then photocopies it and distributes it to a couple of dozen colleagues.

Dijkstra's seminal contribution to programming theory came in 1968, when he was 38 years old. In a short treatise called "Notes on Structured Programming," he argued that most programming is unnecessarily complex because it lacks rigorous mathematical structure. As it happened, many others in the computing community had been worrying for a number of years about the state of software design. With increasing frequency, new software systems for government and industry were costing millions of dollars, running months behind schedule—and still contained thousands of errors when they were finally released. Even as Dijkstra was composing his treatise, the North Atlantic Treaty Organization held a world conference on what it called the "software crisis."

A CALL FOR MATHEMATICAL RIGOR

The principal focus of Dijkstra's criticism was a familiar programming command known as the unconditional jump, or GOTO statement. This command, which transfers control from one point in a program to another, is extremely useful but hampers easy understanding of the program (by humans, that is; computers have no problems following GOTO statements). It is as if the reader of a novel were constantly being instructed to jump back and forth to different pages in the book. By breaking the logical flow, GOTO commands make it practically impossible for someone other than the original programmer to grasp the intricacies of the program well enough to make revisions without introducing errors in unexpected places. As one American computer scientist put it, "If you have lots of GOTOs in a program, that program will be like spaghetti."

To replace GOTO statements, Dijkstra urged the use of three kinds of control structures: simple sequencing, or doing one thing and then doing the next; alternation, in which a program performs one of two or more possible operations; and repetition, in which a program continually performs a single operation as long as a certain condition holds. By using these three structures, he insisted, the programmer could dispense with all GOTOs.

At first, Dijkstra's ideas met with derision from programmers loath to throw away GOTOs. Then, during the early 1970s, an IBM team under computer scientist Harlan Mills used structured programming to create an information bank for *The New York Times*. The work went remarkably smoothly, and the completed program contained practically no bugs.

Since then, structured programming has exerted a profound influence on the development of software ranging from home computer programs to multimillion-dollar defense projects. Several major programming languages, such as Pascal, now incorporate Dijkstra's radical principles. "We can do things that we weren't able to do 10 or 15 years ago," declared Harlan Mills. "I don't think the space shuttle would be flying without structured programming."

A milestone of popular acceptance came in 1975 when John Kemeny and Thomas Kurtz, the authors of that most democratic of tongues, Dartmouth BASIC, revised their language. They incorporated structured features and, as Kemeny and Kurtz remembered, "dropped the GOTO statement overnight, with no regrets." A decade later, the two authors undertook another major overhaul of the language. Kemeny and Kurtz had been unaware of the progress of their brainchild in the marketplace until the early 1980s, when Kurtz happened to use a personal computer for the first time. As a result of BASIC's adoption as the lingua franca of microcomputers—whose limited memory size had required several modifications to the original BASIC—a number of unstructured dialects had come into use. "I was appalled at what I saw," Kurtz said. In conjunction with the American National Standards Institute, or ANSI, Kurtz and Kemeny developed a definitive version for microcomputers, which they called True BASIC.

TRIAL-AND-ERROR TESTING

Edsger Dijkstra, having helped reshape how programs and even languages are written, has continued to be a persistent critic of computing. Testing and debugging, the final phase of software development, galls him as much as the GOTO command. Since the days of batch processing this phase traditionally has been one of trial and error. The complete program is loaded into the computer and tested. If an error is found, it is corrected and the program run again. If another error turns up, that one is corrected and the process repeated. Carried out this way, testing and debugging often takes longer than all other phases of program development combined. In addition, as Dijkstra has pointed out, testing can demonstrate only the presence of errors, never their absence. Even after a program seems to have been fully debugged, new input may cause it to fail— "crash," in computer jargon.

Instead of testing programs, Dijkstra wants to verify them through the application of mathematical principles. He has succeeded with very small programs, but not with big ones. As programs grow larger, the length of the mathematical proof required becomes unmanageable—as long as the program itself, and as error-prone. Dijkstra believes that, to prove large programs, mathematicians and computer scientists will have to "increase our powers of reasoning by an order of magnitude." He admits that goal is ambitious—"but it is not necessarily unrealistic."

In the long run, many computer scientists want to change other phases of software development as well. One important goal in the crusade against complexity is to standardize individual parts of programs in a manner similar to the creation of libraries of subroutines, so that they are as interchangeable as pieces of hardware. No longer would the software developer have to build every system from scratch. Like an engineer fitting together memory chips and other existing hardware to make a computer, the programmer could build a whole new system with modules of software right off the shelf.

The Programmer's Exacting Art

The task of writing a computer program is humbling in its rigor. Computers demand absolute completeness and precision in their instructions: They do only what they are told — and their orders cannot contain the least ambiguity. This is true for all software; it applies equally to a simple program that makes a desktop computer play a tune and to a prodigiously complex program that monitors traffic at an airport.

Writing software would be doubly daunting if it had to be done in the ones and zeros of binary code. At the most basic level, this is the only communication that a computer understands, but programmers have created specialized languages that enable them to construct a set of commands for the machine without dealing directly with strings of binary digits. Many of these so-called high-level languages exist, each with a distinctive grammar and syntax, and each intended for particular sorts of tasks. None can claim all-around utility. For example, a language designed for scientific applications does not readily lend itself to the writing of a program for managing a payroll data base. It could be done, but the programmer would have to invent specialized commands that would be already built into a business-oriented language.

Choosing a suitable high-level language is thus the first step in creating software. Next, the programmer must express the job the computer will do — and the method of doing it — in the form of an algorithm, or step-by-step plan of action. The logic of the algorithm must be faultless or the program will produce gibberish — or simply fail to run.

Finally, the programmer has to consider the types of data the computer will be handling and decide on the best methods for storing the data and retrieving it for processing. If the program must respond to activities in which time is critical — monitoring a reaction in a chemical factory, say — the best methods will be the fastest. But in other circumstances — a program to maintain the records of a bank's loan department, for example — methods that guarantee data security and efficient access to data stored on disks will generally be better than those that are concerned only with rapid processing.

As illustrated on the following pages, programmers have devised a number of strategies and techniques that help them create software for a wide spectrum of human problems and endeavors. By making the right decisions regarding language, logic and programming techniques, they can harness the power of the computer with maximum effectiveness.

The Perils of Imprecision

Although it would be convenient to be able to give them instructions in normal English, French, Chinese or any other natural language, computers are simply too inflexible to understand the subtleties of human communication. In conversation, people supplement their words with gestures and facial expressions. They use exaggeration, understatement, sarcasm and other rhetorical devices to communicate one thing while saying another. They employ words with multiple meanings, trusting context, inflection, body language and other factors to clarify what they intend to say. Even in written communication, human beings use all sorts of cues to decipher the messages in one another's statements.

"This car is hot," someone says. If the speaker is an automobile dealer, the listener understands that the car is popular. The same statement from a police officer means that the vehicle is stolen. From a driver who had just completed a 100-mile journey on a 100° F. day, the sentence warns listeners not to burn their fingers by touching the car.

Human intelligence can solve the puzzle of natural language, but a computer requires a rigid, mathematically precise communication system: Each symbol or group of symbols must mean exactly the same thing every time, and every statement is to be taken literally. There can be no such thing as irony, colloquialism or shades of meaning.

Natural human languages are full of words that vary their meaning according to context. Unlike a computer, a person would quickly understand that an instruction to "file the papers" refers to storing them in a file drawer — not rasping them with a tool.

Natural language communication often relies on a culturally learned shorthand. A computer would not know, for example, that "I'll have coffee with my cereal" means "I'll have a cup of coffee as well as a bowl of cereal," not "I'll have coffee mixed in with my cereal."

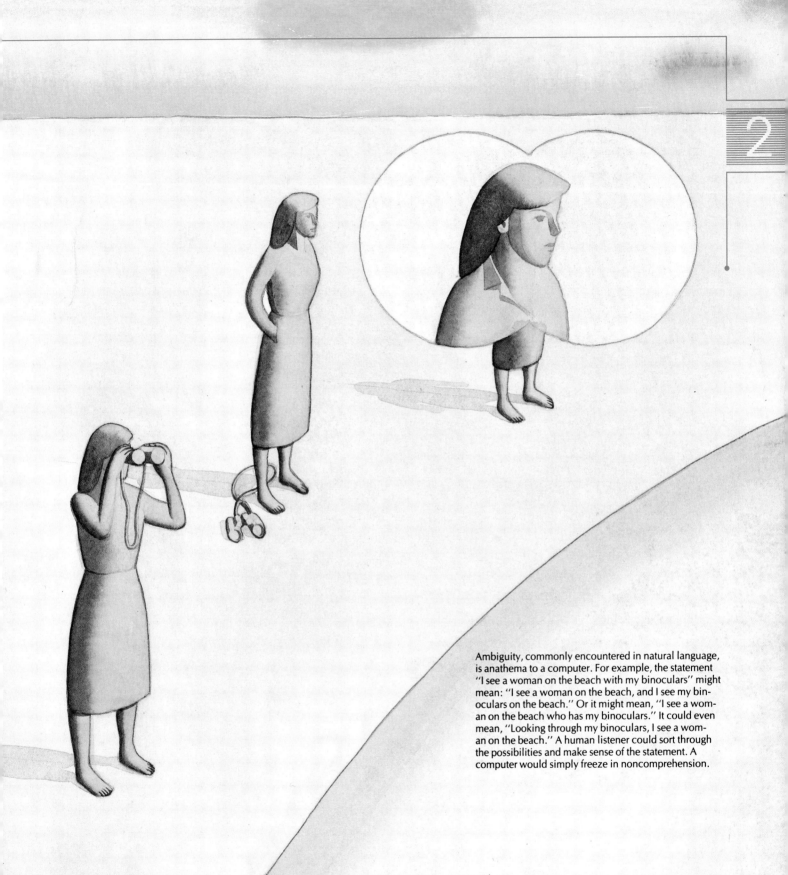

Ambiguity, commonly encountered in natural language, is anathema to a computer. For example, the statement "I see a woman on the beach with my binoculars" might mean: "I see a woman on the beach, and I see my binoculars on the beach." Or it might mean, "I see a woman on the beach who has my binoculars." It could even mean, "Looking through my binoculars, I see a woman on the beach." A human listener could sort through the possibilities and make sense of the statement. A computer would simply freeze in noncomprehension.

Hard-working Translator Programs

At root, a computer responds to instructions and data only when they are framed in machine code — a language of ones and zeros that meshes directly with that particular computer's circuitry. However, writing a program in machine code is a mind-numbing task. Slightly less tedious to use is assembly language, a low-level language that employs short mnemonic codes instead of zeros and ones (STA, for example, might tell the computer to store something in the accumulator). Another program, called an assembler, translates an assembly program into machine code. Like machine code, assembly language is machine-specific, and both allow the programmer to make the most efficient use of a given computer's circuitry.

Most programmers prefer to use higher-level languages such as BASIC or COBOL because they are much closer to

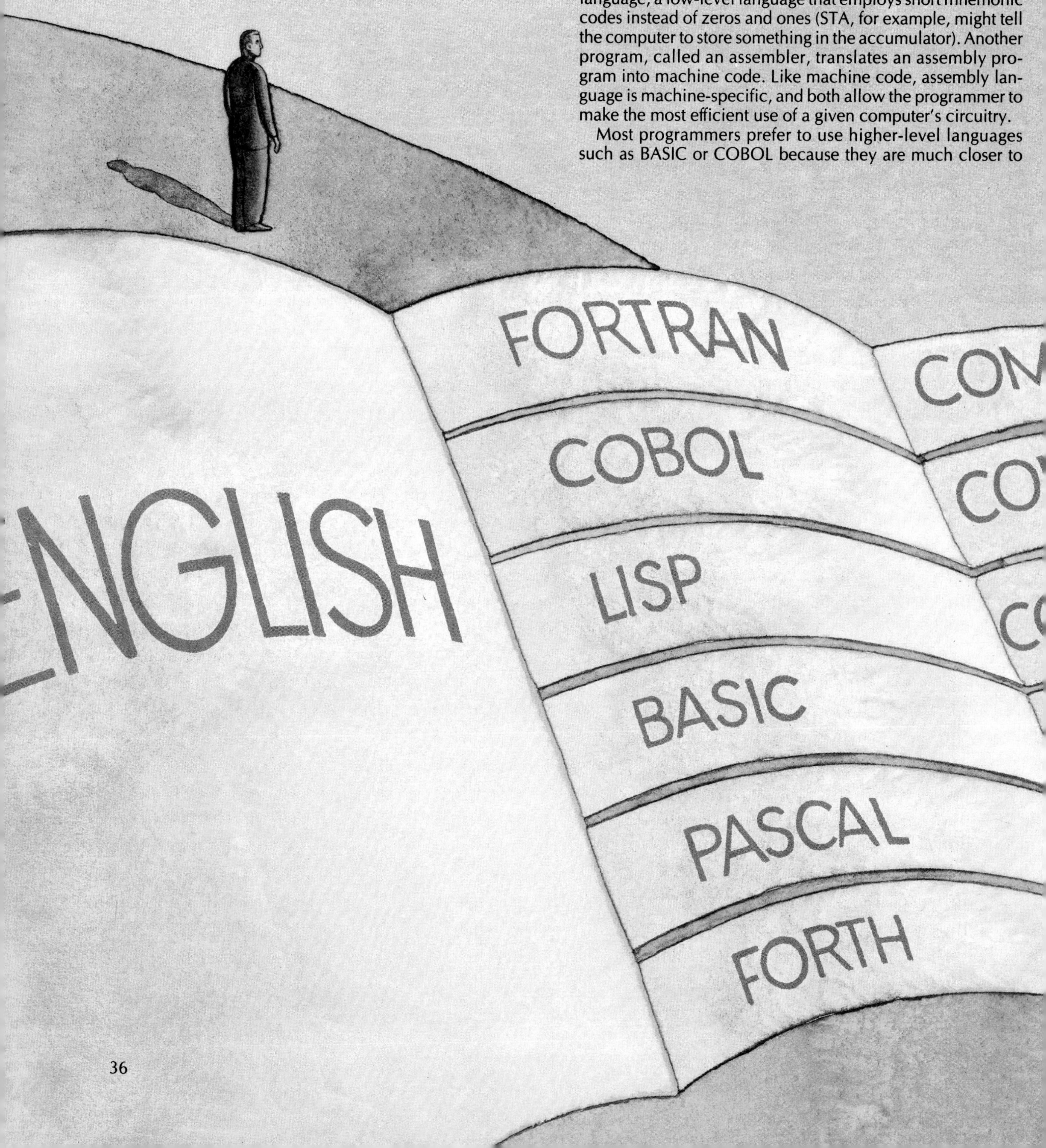

ENGLISH

FORTRAN

COBOL

LISP

BASIC

PASCAL

FORTH

COM

CO

CO

natural human language. Still, a computer cannot carry out any instructions until they have been translated into zeros and ones. This translation may be done by a compiler or an interpreter, special programs tailored to both the language and the machine being used. Usually these translators are loaded into temporary memory from external storage, but in some systems, an interpreter is stored in permanent memory.

The two translators have different modes of operation. A compiler reads an entire program, makes a translation and produces a complete machine language version, which is then loaded into the computer and executed. An interpreter translates and executes the program one line at a time. Once a program is compiled, neither the original program nor the compiler is needed. But a program written in an interpreted language must be interpreted each time it is run. Compiled programs thus run faster, but interpreted programs are easier to correct or modify.

A given language is either compiled or interpreted, depending on the use for which it was invented. FORTRAN, for example, was created to handle large programs for scientific and mathematical applications where speed of execution is paramount; thus, FORTRAN is usually implemented with a compiler. BASIC, on the other hand, was intended for use by novice programmers, for whom the line-by-line execution of an interpreter is invaluable. In some cases, both compilers and interpreters are available for the same language; this means a program may be developed using an interpreter for testing and then compiled for greater speed.

Matching the Language to the Job

Asking a dozen programmers to name the best computer language is likely to elicit a dozen different answers, for there is no best computer language, any more than one natural human language is superior to all the rest. Theoretically, most programming tasks could be accomplished with any language, but writing a program for a given job is actually considerably easier in some languages than in others, since the way a computer language expresses ideas was shaped with particular programming needs in mind.

Programming languages each have a special vocabulary of so-called keywords — words, letters, numbers or other symbols. The keywords correspond to particular operations or sequences of operations to be performed by the computer. Some of them function as verbs, and others function as nouns, modifiers or punctuation marks. They are strung together according to the rules of syntax in the language to form the programming equivalents of sentences. In selecting the most appropriate language for a programming job, several factors must be taken into consideration, among them the programmer's level of experience and the size of the program to be written. BASIC is relatively easy to learn and well suited to devising short, simple programs; however, long programs in BASIC can be unwieldy and difficult to organize. Pascal gives coherence to long programs, imposing a strict logical structure that is valued by serious novices for the discipline it teaches them. For short programs, however, Pascal may be too cumbersome.

Other important considerations include the program's speed and ease of maintenance — that is, the ease with which a program can be altered, enhanced, updated and debugged once it is in use. Programs written in FORTH, an extremely terse language, take up little space in memory; several keywords in FORTH are simply punctuation marks. This allows FORTH programs to run quite fast compared with programs written in BASIC, but it also makes them difficult to read and maintain. COBOL programs, on the other hand, are especially easy to maintain. Not only are they divided into four distinct parts — describing the program's purpose, the computer the program was written for, the type of data used and the processing instructions — they also follow a syntax modeled on that of the English sentence.

```
*(DE CELSIUS(X) ( *QUO(  x 32) 1.8) )
   CELSIUS
*(EVAL ' (CELSIUS 104) )
   40.0

*
```

```
10 INPUT "What is your name?"; N$
20 PRINT "Hello," ;N$
30 END
```

LISP (list processing) is widely used in artificial intelligence research, the branch of computer science concerned with programming computers to imitate human thought. Created in the late 1950s by M.I.T. mathematician John McCarthy, LISP is better suited to the task of manipulating symbols than to ordinary number crunching.

This program converts Fahrenheit to Celsius.

BASIC (beginners all-purpose symbolic instruction code) is often the first computer language learned by schoolchildren and other novice programmers. It was created in the mid-1960s by Dartmouth College professors John Kemeny and Thomas Kurtz, and gained popularity in the following decade as a language compact enough to fit in the limited memories of early personal computers.

This is a very short name game.

```
        SUM = 0.0
C Compute the average of a set of values
        DO 100 I = 1,LAST
100     SUM = SUM + A (I)
        AVER = SUM / LAST
```

```
PRINT-AMOUNT-ON-CHECK.
    MOVE EMPLOYEE-AMOUNT-TO-BE-PAID
        TO CHECK-DOLLAR-AND-CENTS-AMOUNT.
    MOVE EMPLOYEE-AMOUNT-TO-BE-PAID
        TO WORK-TOTAL-AMOUNT.
    MOVE WORK-DOLLAR-AMOUNT
        TO CHECK-DOLLAR-AMOUNT.
```

FORTRAN (from formula translator) was created in the mid-1950s by IBM programmers. Used especially for programs involving scientific and mathematical calculations, FORTRAN has had a long-term influence: "In a sense," one computer scientist has declared, "all programming language research since 1957 has been motivated by attempts to correct flaws in FORTRAN."

This program computes a numerical average.

COBOL (common business oriented language) was born at the Pentagon in 1960, the product of a joint effort by the federal government and the computer industry. Designed to be easily understood by nonscientists in the business world, the language uses an English-like structure and vocabulary. It is the most popular data-processing language in such institutions as banks and insurance companies.

This is a section of a check-writing program.

```
VAR
    message : STRING;
BEGIN
    message: = 'I think
    therefore I am.';
    writeln(message);
END.
```

```
7 2 * 5 + .19ok
```

Pascal, named for 17th Century French mathematician Blaise Pascal, was designed by Swiss computer scientist Niklaus Wirth. Regarded as a vital tool for learning the discipline of structured programming, Pascal has since 1983 been the required language for American high-school students taking advanced placement exams in computer science.

This program tells the computer to print out, "I think therefore I am."

FORTH (originally named Fourth for "fourth generation computer language") was the brainchild of programmer Charles Moore, who designed the language in the late 1960s and early 1970s as a personal tool for increasing his own productivity. FORTH became more widely used for control applications after Moore employed it to write the software controlling the radio telescope at an Arizona observatory.

This program computes 5 + (2 x 7).

Commands for Manipulating Data

By using a given set of commands, a program tells a computer exactly what to do with each item of information being processed, in much the same way that the figures in the illustrations on these pages are moved through an imaginary school system according to predetermined rules. Certain commands — those controlling input and output of data, for example — are found in virtually every program; others might

INPUT. Students entering school represent data entering the computer in response to an input command. Typing on the computer's keyboard is one of several input methods. The computer can also read data from a disk or other storage medium, and can receive input over the telephone.

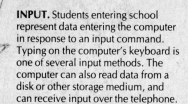

JUMP. From the testing room, students go to await their grades. This represents the jump command (called GOTO in BASIC), which tells the computer to execute some part of the program other than the next consecutive line. Advocates of structured programming seek to eliminate GOTOs because they make programs difficult to decipher.

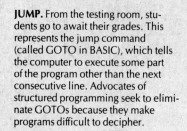

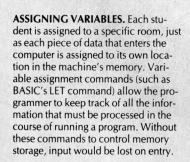

ASSIGNING VARIABLES. Each student is assigned to a specific room, just as each piece of data that enters the computer is assigned to its own location in the machine's memory. Variable assignment commands (such as BASIC's LET command) allow the programmer to keep track of all the information that must be processed in the course of running a program. Without these commands to control memory storage, input would be lost on entry.

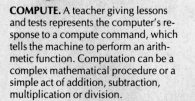

COMPUTE. A teacher giving lessons and tests represents the computer's response to a compute command, which tells the machine to perform an arithmetic function. Computation can be a complex mathematical procedure or a simple act of addition, subtraction, multiplication or division.

be omitted from a very simple program. But all seven actions depicted below are so fundamental that it would be unusual to find a program of any significant power or complexity that did not incorporate all of them.

Programmers do not have to use these commands in the sequence illustrated here. Input and output, for example, can occur not only at the beginning and end of a program but also at any point in between. The other commands can be arranged in any sequence and repeated as many times as necessary within a particular program. Because they are indispensable to programmers, these commands are common to all computer languages. They are written differently in each language but always control the same computing actions.

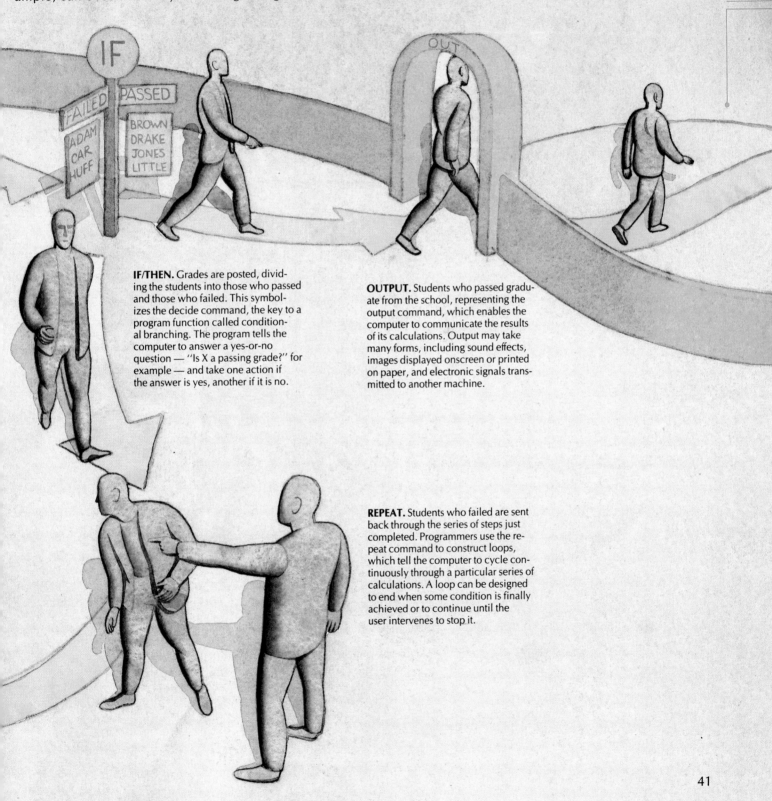

IF/THEN. Grades are posted, dividing the students into those who passed and those who failed. This symbolizes the decide command, the key to a program function called conditional branching. The program tells the computer to answer a yes-or-no question — "Is X a passing grade?" for example — and take one action if the answer is yes, another if it is no.

OUTPUT. Students who passed graduate from the school, representing the output command, which enables the computer to communicate the results of its calculations. Output may take many forms, including sound effects, images displayed onscreen or printed on paper, and electronic signals transmitted to another machine.

REPEAT. Students who failed are sent back through the series of steps just completed. Programmers use the repeat command to construct loops, which tell the computer to cycle continuously through a particular series of calculations. A loop can be designed to end when some condition is finally achieved or to continue until the user intervenes to stop it.

Devising a Plan of Action

A programmer's goal is not to solve a problem but to map out instructions that will let the computer find the solution. Given its speed at manipulating numbers, a computer is well suited to solving problems that involve difficult or repetitive calculations. As illustrated in the simulated computer program here and on the following five pages, the machine is also capable of dealing with problems that can be expressed in the if/then statements of formal logic or as sequences of true/false options.

If performing rapid calculations is a job tailor-made for a computer, the more thoughtful task of designing the step-by-step recipe, or algorithm, that tells a computer exactly how to proceed with a given assignment is better left to human intelligence. In order to make the algorithm as clear and concise as possible, a programmer always starts by assembling the known facts and setting out a clear statement of the problem. Only then would the programmer begin devising a logical progression of steps for the computer to follow en route to the solution.

After formulating the necessary algorithm, the programmer's next challenge is to translate each step into precise instructions according to the rules of whichever computer language has been chosen. Often the programmer will then use an extreme version of the problem just to see if the logic of the algorithm holds up. This test often discovers missing steps or inaccurate instructions that would cause the computer to flash error messages.

No detail, however self-evident to the human mind, can be omitted or taken for granted in a computer program. A good programmer must be capable of both the big-picture thinking that conceives useful algorithms and the minute attention to detail that converts those algorithms into unambiguous computer code.

This demonstration of the process of designing a computer program begins with the declaration of a fanciful problem. The box at right represents the outermost in a group of nested red lacquered boxes, which fit snugly one inside the other, with no space between their walls. At the heart of the nest of boxes is a priceless emerald hidden there by an emperor. Exactly one inch in diameter, the fabulous jewel is enclosed in the smallest box capable of holding it. Each of the boxes — from the largest one, which is 10 feet on each side, to the innermost one, which holds the emerald — has walls one quarter inch thick. The emperor has promised the emerald to the first person who figures out how many boxes have to be opened to reach the jewel.

NOTES:

— Restate the problem
   How many boxes must be opened
   to reach the jewel?

— State the given facts.
   The size of the outer box -- 10 feet
      on a side
   The wall thickness -- ¼ inch thick
   The size of the jewel -- 1 inch in
      diameter (This dictates the
      size of the smallest box.)
   The size of the smallest
      box -- It must
      measure at least
      1½ inches on a side
      on the outside.

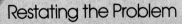

LOGIC OF STEPS (Method)

   Given the dimensions of the box
   and the jewel, the procedure to
   solve the problem is to keep sub-
   tracting double the wall thickness
   (½ inch) from the outer box as
   long as the result is greater than
   or equal to the smallest possible
   box. The number of times this is
   required is the answer to the
   problem.

① Restating the Problem

The programmer's work begins with these preliminary notes. The first step in creating a computer program is to restate the problem in its essential terms, including only the facts that are relevant to its solution. In this case, such details as the color of the boxes and the value of the emerald have no bearing on the problem. The only facts that concern the programmer are the size of the jewel, the thickness of the box walls and the dimensions of the largest box. Applying logic and ingenuity to these few facts, the programmer begins to sketch out a method for finding a solution.

INPUTS
  BIGGEST (the outer size of the biggest box)
  THICKNESS (the thickness of the walls)
  JEWEL (the size of the jewel)

OUTPUTS
  COUNT (how many boxes were opened)
  Error messages — Show error message
  if the COUNT comes out to 0, if the
  THICKNESS is less than or equal to
  (< =) 0, if the JEWEL is less than
  or equal to (< =) 0.

WHAT TO DO
  INPUT — BIGGEST, THICKNESS, JEWEL
  Given the INPUTS, test that the
  problem is solvable.
  If successful initialize. Begin the
  procedure by putting the following
  variables into the computer's
  memory:

  ```
  COUNT ← 0
  THISBOX ← BIGGEST
  SMALLEST ← JEWEL SIZE + 2 x THICKNESS
  ```

  Repeat while THISBOX > = SMALLEST BOX
  THISBOX ← THISBOX − (2 x THICKNESS)
  COUNT ← COUNT + 1

  OUTPUT COUNT and/or error messages.

Devising the Algorithm

To determine the steps of the solution, the programmer first decides what information the computer needs, giving these INPUT variables code names for easy reference. Next, the programmer determines the information the computer will display. These OUTPUTS in-clude error messages so the computer will warn of incorrect or illogical INPUTS. Finally, the programmer designs the algorithm, us-ing the ← symbol to assign values to key vari-ables such as THISBOX, the dimension of the new box uncovered at each opening.

BIGGEST BOX = 6 INCHES
WALL THICKNESS = .25 INCHES
JEWEL SIZE = 1 INCH

6 − .50 = 5.50	COUNT 1
5.50 − .50 = 5	COUNT 2
5 − .50 = 4.50	COUNT 3
4.50 − .50 = 4	COUNT 4
4 − .50 = 3.50	COUNT 5
3.50 − .50 = 3	COUNT 6
3 − .50 = 2.50	COUNT 7
2.50 − .50 = 2	COUNT 8
2 − .50 = 1.5	COUNT 9
1.5 IS THE	COUNT 10
SMALLEST POSSIBLE	
BOX	

This works.

BIGGEST BOX = .1 FOOT
WALL THICKNESS = .25 INCHES
JEWEL SIZE = 1 INCH

Since the smallest possible box
is 1.5, the value of the biggest
box makes the problem impossible
to solve. The problem is solvable
only if the biggest box is larger
than 1.5 inches.

Running a Test

To find out whether the logic of the algorithm is sound, the programmer runs two simple tests, assigning values to the INPUT variables and carrying out the program by hand. The algorithm will work as long as the outermost box is larger than the emerald.

```
10    INPUT "How big is the outer box (in inches)";BIGGEST
20    INPUT "How thick are the walls of the box (decimal fractions of an inch)";
         THICKNESS
30    INPUT "How big is the jewel (in inches)";JEWEL
40    IF THICKNESS <= 0 OR JEWEL <= 0 THEN PRINT "You gotta be kidding . . .":
         END
50    IF BIGGEST < JEWEL + (2 * THICKNESS) THEN PRINT "The outer box is WAY
         too small to hold the jewel" :END
60    LET COUNT = 0
70    LET SMALLEST = JEWEL + (2 * THICKNESS)
80    LET THISBOX = BIGGEST
90    REM this is the part that repeats . . .
100   WHILE THISBOX >= SMALLEST
110   LET THISBOX = THISBOX - (2 * THICKNESS)
120   LET COUNT = COUNT + 1
130   PRINT "I am opening one more box.";COUNT;" so far . . ."
140   WEND : REM The while statement ends here
150   PRINT "We have opened a total of ";COUNT;" boxes."
160   END
      RUN
```

Writing the Program

The program on the screen is written in BA-SIC, with lines numbered by tens so that additional steps may be inserted if necessary. INPUT lines tell the computer to ask for the fixed values that define the problem; LET tells it to give certain variables values that will change as the program is run. The computer will ignore any line beginning with REM, which programmers use to write remarks to themselves. Lines 100-140 form the heart of the program — a loop that the computer will repeat until it reaches the solution.

(5)

Running the Program

Once the program is entered into the computer, the programmer has only to type the command RUN and the machine will go to work, mathematically opening boxes by repeating the subtraction loop spelled out in the program. The programmer can now restate the problem and its solution: A one-inch jewel is inside the smallest possible box inside a nest of boxes with no space between them. The boxes have walls one quarter inch thick. The largest box is 10 feet on a side. To reach the jewel, 238 boxes must be opened.

A Visual Chart of the Process

A useful tool of programming is a flow chart, a graphic representation of the invisible system designed by the programmer. By employing standard symbols for various parts of a program *(below)*, it provides an easy-to-read map of the step-by-step process the machine is being instructed to carry out. Often programmers will outline their algorithms in flow-chart form as a way to organize their thoughts before they begin writing the more formal code required by a programming language. Once the program is written, the chart can also act as a check to make sure no essential steps have been omitted.

Although detailed charts with many decision paths are sometimes laborious to draw, a flow chart's graphic format is particularly valuable when several programmers are collaborating on a large project. The chart provides a visual reminder of how each individual contribution fits into the overall structure. The United States government, IBM and many other large organizations require programmers to document all their work with flow charts.

The flow chart on the opposite page diagrams the program used to solve the hidden jewel problem. It traces the program's logical flow, from the user's input of the essential numbers through the final display of the solution on the screen. Each time the computer has to make a decision, the flow chart branches in two directions, representing the computer's choice of yes/no or true/false options. Often one choice will feed the program back through a loop.

According to instructions in the rectangular output symbol at the bottom of the chart, the computer will flash changing numbers on the screen as long as the program is looping, to indicate the number of boxes that have been opened thus far. When the jewel is finally uncovered and the program escapes from the loop, the latest running count figure will be presented as the solution.

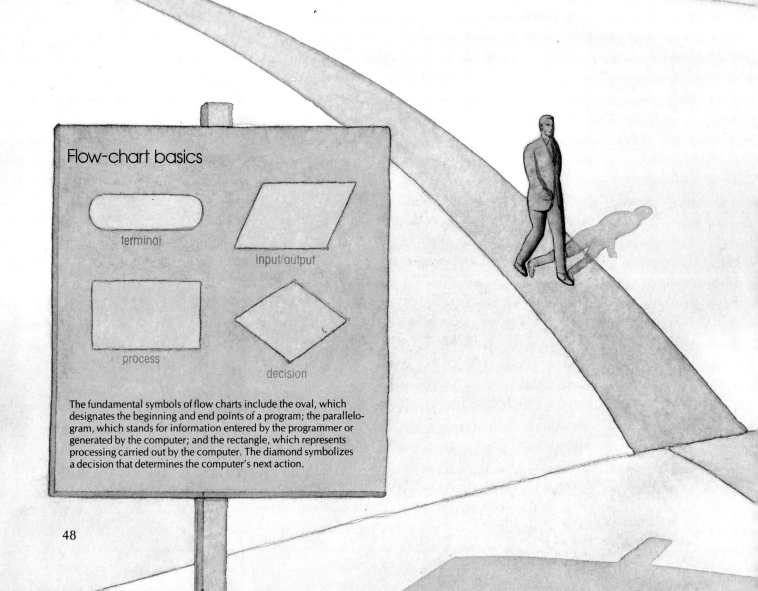

Flow-chart basics

terminal

input/output

process

decision

The fundamental symbols of flow charts include the oval, which designates the beginning and end points of a program; the parallelogram, which stands for information entered by the programmer or generated by the computer; and the rectangle, which represents processing carried out by the computer. The diamond symbolizes a decision that determines the computer's next action.

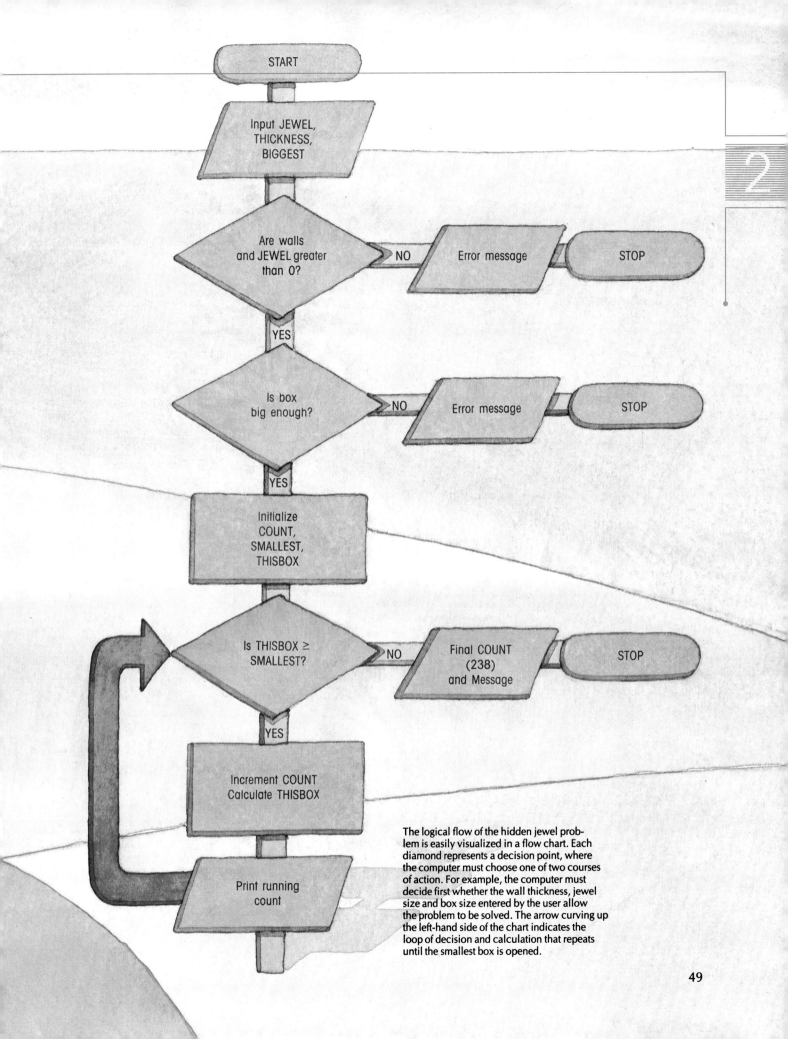

The logical flow of the hidden jewel problem is easily visualized in a flow chart. Each diamond represents a decision point, where the computer must choose one of two courses of action. For example, the computer must decide first whether the wall thickness, jewel size and box size entered by the user allow the problem to be solved. The arrow curving up the left-hand side of the chart indicates the loop of decision and calculation that repeats until the smallest box is opened.

49

Creating Order Out of Randomness

In addition to providing a logical progression of step-by-step instructions for the computer to follow, a computer program must also ensure that the data entered for processing is arranged in an orderly fashion in the computer's memory. Without software techniques to organize the enormous quantities of data the machines are required to store and process, com-

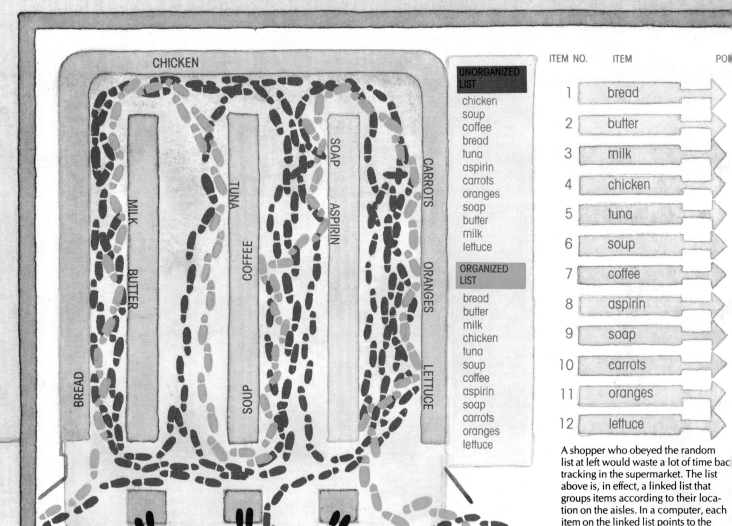

ITEM NO.	ITEM	PO
1	bread	
2	butter	
3	milk	
4	chicken	
5	tuna	
6	soup	
7	coffee	
8	aspirin	
9	soap	
10	carrots	
11	oranges	
12	lettuce	

UNORGANIZED LIST

chicken
soup
coffee
bread
tuna
aspirin
carrots
oranges
soap
butter
milk
lettuce

ORGANIZED LIST

bread
butter
milk
chicken
tuna
soup
coffee
aspirin
soap
carrots
oranges
lettuce

A shopper who obeyed the random list at left would waste a lot of time backtracking in the supermarket. The list above is, in effect, a linked list that groups items according to their location on the aisles. In a computer, each item on the linked list points to the location of the next item.

Lists and Linked Lists

One method of storing information in a computer's memory is a linked list, which preserves the correct order of items through the use of pointers — storage codes that point to the memory location of the next item on the list. Because the items remain linked by pointers, the computer need not store them in a continuous block of memory. Another feature of

linked lists is that individual items can be added or remov without recopying the entire list. Thus, in a word-processi program, for example, the characters that constitute a do ument could be treated as items on a list, allowing the u to make insertions or deletions anywhere in the docume without disturbing the order of the other words.

puters would be virtually useless. It would be as difficult to use a computer without organizing software as it would be to look something up in an encyclopedia or a dictionary that listed its entries entirely at random, rather than imposing on them the structure of alphabetical order.

Programmers use a number of techniques for organizing information and tucking it away in the computer's memory. These methods must also allow the computer to retrieve the information when necessary. Often, as shown here and on the following pages, these techniques are described in terms of familiar phenomena from the physical world, such as stacks, queues and lists.

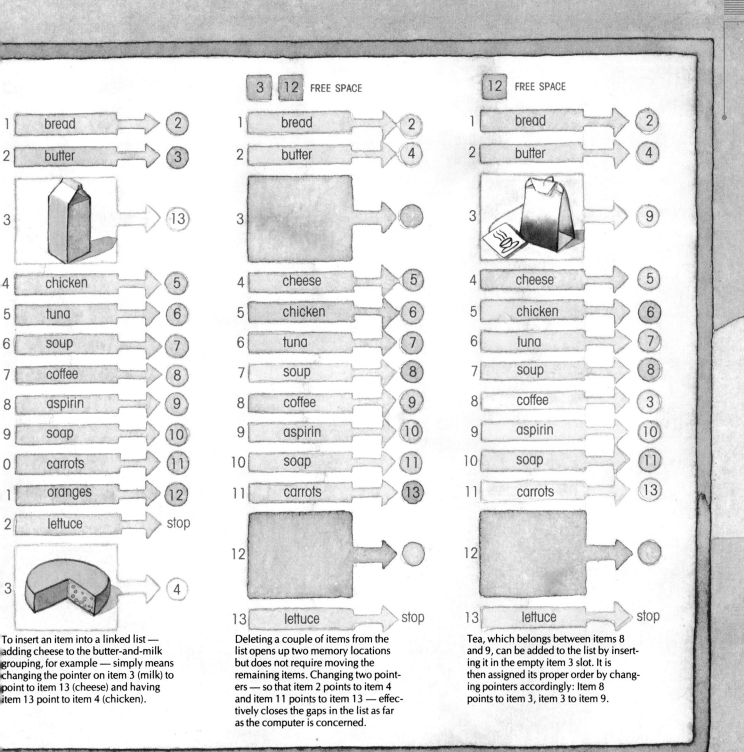

To insert an item into a linked list — adding cheese to the butter-and-milk grouping, for example — simply means changing the pointer on item 3 (milk) to point to item 13 (cheese) and having item 13 point to item 4 (chicken).

Deleting a couple of items from the list opens up two memory locations but does not require moving the remaining items. Changing two pointers — so that item 2 points to item 4 and item 11 points to item 13 — effectively closes the gaps in the list as far as the computer is concerned.

Tea, which belongs between items 8 and 9, can be added to the list by inserting it in the empty item 3 slot. It is then assigned its proper order by changing pointers accordingly: Item 8 points to item 3, item 3 to item 9.

Storing Data for Easy Access

A critical factor in the smooth running of a program is the arrangement of data so that it is easily available for computation or inspection. Two often-used methods of arranging data go by the acronymns FIFO and LIFO, programming jargon for "first in, first out" and "last in, first out." An escalator, for example, may be thought of as a FIFO device: The first person to board it is also first to step off at the next level. An elevator, on the other hand, often functions as a LIFO device: The first

Queue. To illustrate the storage method called the circular queue, pieces of data are represented as numbered marbles rolling down a chute into the computer's temporary memory. They are routed through the memory along a pathway that preserves their order, so that the first piece of data to enter the memory becomes the first one released for display on the screen.

TO SCREEN

TEMPORARY MEMORY

passengers to enter crowd toward the back, so that the last person aboard is in a position to exit first when the doors open. The FIFO storage method is also referred to as a queue *(opposite)*, while data stored by the LIFO method is said to be in a stack *(below)*.

Programmers use FIFO storage when data must be processed in the order it comes in. A word-processing program, for example, must display letters on the screen in the same order that they are typed on the keyboard. With some programming languages, such as FORTH, LIFO memory stacks are used to handle certain arithmetic functions. In the example below, the computer stacks a problem because it cannot be solved by processing the numbers in the order they were entered: The multiplication portion cannot be carried out until after the addition (in parentheses). The problem has to be solved back to front.

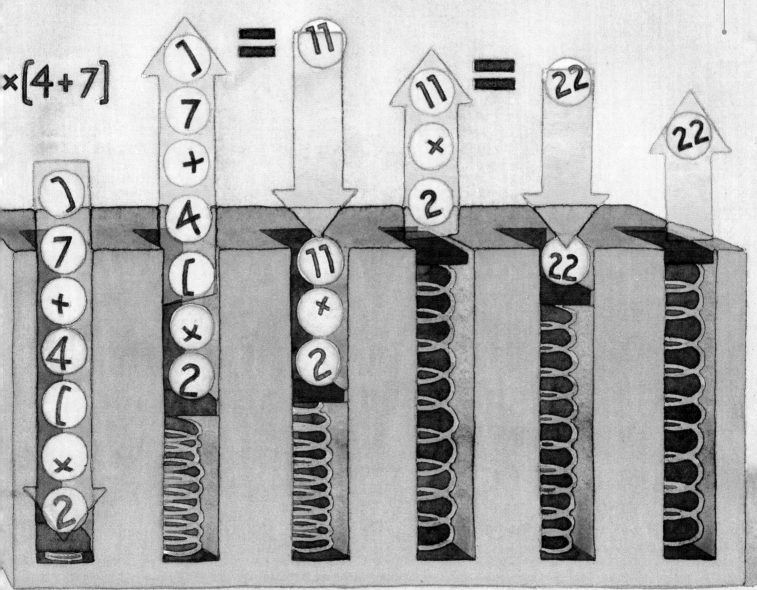

Stack. The numbers and other symbols for this calculation are stacked in the order they are entered.

The addition of 4 and 7 is thus the first operation to pop up for processing.

When computation is finished, the sum, 11, drops back onto the stack.

Next in line for processing is the multiplication of 2 by 11.

The product of that calculation, 22, drops back onto the stack.

Now the only item in the stack, 22, is presented as the answer.

Techniques for Sorts and Searches

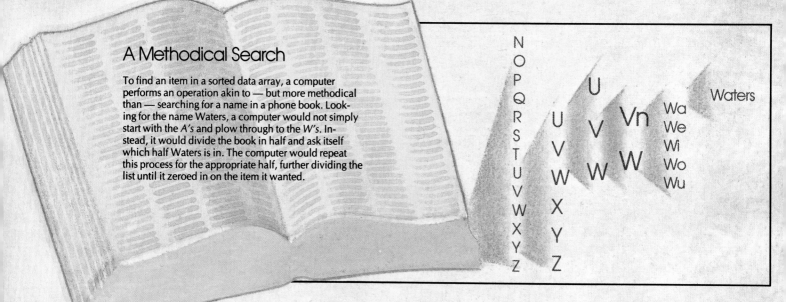

Sorting lists of data into manageable order is such an important computing function — and has become such an art within the world of programming — that programs have been created especially to do the job. When writing any kind of program in which sorting will be required, programmers can wait until the rest of the program is finished and simply select the most appropriate method.

Two popular techniques are illustrated here. Bubble sorting gets its name from the fact that some of the items being sorted rise through the list like bubbles through liquid. In the drawing at right, the runner named Alex is depicted as rising to the top of an alphabetical list. A bubble-sorting program works its way down a list, comparing the first and second items, then the second and third, and so on, reversing the members of each pair if they are not in the correct order with respect to each other. When it reaches the bottom of the list, the program returns to the top and moves downward again, repeating the process until all the items are in their proper place.

A bin-sorting program puts items into imaginary bins — one for each letter, for example, if the list is being sorted alphabetically — then divides each bin into sub-bins and keeps sorting until each item is in a bin of its own. For some long lists, a combination of the two techniques can be more efficient than either of them alone. First the entire list is bin-sorted, then each bin is individually bubble-sorted.

The names of the runners in this marathon make up a list that must be sorted into alphabetical order. A sample of six runners selected from the field is used to demonstrate three sorting methods. To alphabetize by bubble sorting alone, the computer makes 12 comparing and switching moves. To bin-sort takes eight moves, into three bins and five sub-bins. A combination of bin and bubble sorting takes only six moves.

The bubble-sorting program starts by comparing the first two names on the list — Bill and Ann — and switching the order (1). Bill, now item two on the list, is then compared with Betty and switched (2) to become item three. The program compares item three with item four: no switch (3). Bob, item four, is then compared and switched with Alex (4) and then with Carl: no switch (5). On each subsequent pass through the list, the program moves Alex up one space until the list has been sorted into order.

A Methodical Search

To find an item in a sorted data array, a computer performs an operation akin to — but more methodical than — searching for a name in a phone book. Looking for the name Waters, a computer would not simply start with the A's and plow through to the W's. Instead, it would divide the book in half and ask itself which half Waters is in. The computer would repeat this process for the appropriate half, further dividing the list until it zeroed in on the item it wanted.

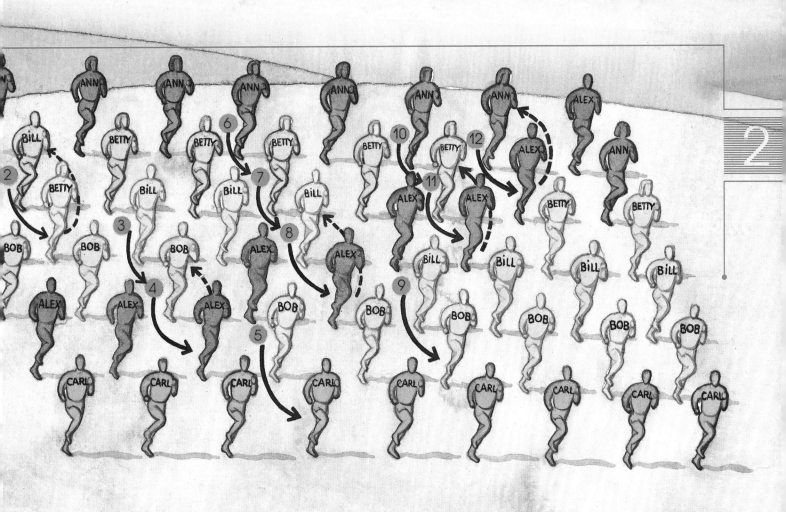

A bin-sorting program promptly puts Ann and Alex into the A bin; Bill, Betty and Bob into the B bin; and Carl into the C bin. The A bin is then subdivided into Al and An bins, and the B bin into sub-bins Be, Bi and Bo. Since no subdividing is required in the C bin, the sort is complete after eight steps. If there had been an Alice in the Al bin with Alex, or a Ben in the Be bin with Betty, more moves would have been needed.

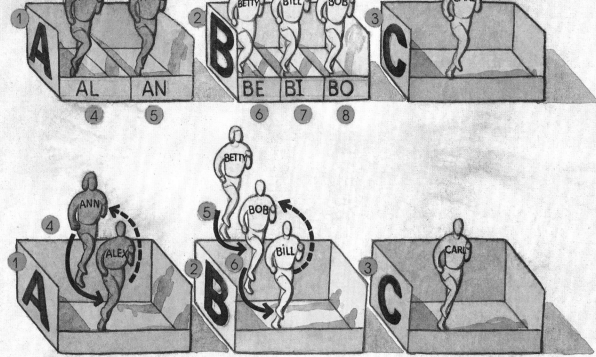

The most efficient way to alphabetize the list is a combination sort that starts by putting the six runners into three bins, then switches to bubble sorting. In bins A and B, the runners are sorted in three compare-and-switch moves instead of five moves to create five sub-bins. Again, the C bin needs no further sorting, so the job is complete in six steps.

The Software Explosion

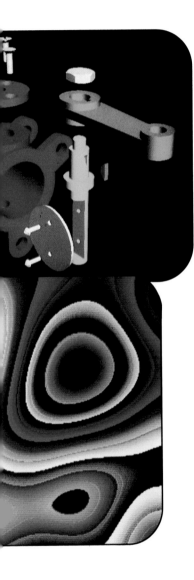

The cover story of the January 1975 *Popular Electronics* was an electrifying one for computer enthusiasts. The first of a two-part series, it described the "World's First Minicomputer Kit to Rival Commercial Models . . . Altair 8800." Within days, hundreds of people had sent off their checks for $397 to the manufacturer, a small Albuquerque, New Mexico, company called Micro Instrumentation and Telemetry Systems—MITS for short.

Assembling the kit was not easy, despite its minimalist nature. The finished computer consisted of a single microchip housed in a small blue box whose front panel bore rows of switches and indicator lights, but even experienced electronics hobbyists had to spend hours wiring it. Once the machines were assembled, owners had once again to draw heavily on their own resources. The Altair came with no software, and none was available commercially. The user who actually wanted the machine to do something had to supply an original program.

To work in the Altair, such a program had to meet two requirements. First, it had to be short. The Altair's central processing unit had a 256-byte memory, enough to hold only about a paragraph of information. Second, the program had to be composed in the zeros and ones of machine code. After writing this short binary-coded program, the Altair user then had to enter it into the computer by laboriously setting the toggle switches—one switch per binary digit—on the front of the machine. Output was signaled by a cryptic display of lights that users had to learn to decode. All in all, the Altair was not for the timid.

Among the venturesome tinkerers who fired off their money to get their hands on the first Altairs were many who would, before the decade was out, help foment a revolution in the computer industry. Building on their experience with this rudimentary machine, some would design smaller and better computers; others would write imaginative programs capable of performing tasks—such as graphics editing and complex financial analysis—undreamed of just a few years before. But when they first put their hands on the Altair, they were throwbacks of a sort, throwbacks to the earliest days of electronic computers, when programmers had to be intimately familiar with a machine's inner workings before they could devise software that would make the computer productive. As John Backus, one of the creators of the high-level computer language FORTRAN, said of those pioneering times, the programmer "had to be a resourceful inventor to adapt his problem to the idiosyncrasies of the computer. He had to fit his program and data into a tiny store, and overcome bizarre difficulties in getting information in and out of it, all while using a limited and often peculiar set of instructions." But Altair buyers also had an advantage over the first generation of programmers, for computer hardware and software had both taken giant strides since the days

57

when changing programs in mammoth machines such as ENIAC and the Harvard Mark I was something that could be done only by a computer technician.

The proliferation of computers during the 1950s and early 1960s, particularly at major universities, had put the machines within reach of a new breed of programmer. Earlier programmers, working for corporations or institutions, were generally most interested in carrying out complex mathematical computations or improving the management of such things as payrolls or student registration. The newcomers, however, were simply fascinated by the process of computing. Most of them were students, some of them electronics hobbyists, and there was nothing they liked better than pushing the limits of what a computer could do.

These computer addicts chafed at the batch-processing restrictions that called for handing over their programs to computer operators and waiting hours for the results. So the rebels found other ways to get at a computer. First they looked for a physics or math department with its own minicomputer; such machines could be programmed with punched paper tape and were instantly responsive to commands typed in at a keyboard. Next, they signed up for computer time in the name of someone entitled to access, or they sneaked into empty computer rooms at night or on weekends. "You could roll in at 9 p.m. when the physicists had left," one of them later said, "and you could stay there till 9 a.m. when they rolled back in. Do it night after night. I made it to classes but I slept through them."

HACKING'S BIRTHPLACE

Possibly the original hotbed of such compulsive computing was MIT, where the addicts called themselves hackers. The name, first applied to student pranksters, later attached itself to certain members of the Tech Model Railroad Club. The club was divided into two factions: One group was most interested in the realistic trains and scenery atop the club's sprawling layout; the other was fascinated by the spaghetti-like maze of wiring underneath it—the complex electrical system that made the whole thing work. With the zeal of fanatics, core members of this latter group spent countless hours tinkering with the system, learning how a change here would affect an operation there, marveling at the interrelatedness of it all. They even developed a vocabulary all their own. Ruined equipment was said to be "munged," or mashed until no good; a project with no discernible utility beyond the pleasure taken in its execution was—like earlier practical jokes—a "hack." Inevitably, those who hacked were known as hackers.

It was just a matter of time before the hackers discovered computers. They could gain only limited access to the institute's huge IBM system, but with the delivery in July 1958 of a smaller machine, the TX-0, things began to open up. The TX-0 employed transistors rather than bulky vacuum tubes and was fitted with a first-rate CRT monitor. It also had an audio output device, and even a light pen that enabled the user to "draw" directly on the monitor screen. But above all, the TX-0 did not use the batch processing of the IBM mainframe. For the first time at MIT, a computer enthusiast could actually get his hands on a machine, feed his own program into it on paper tape and get results immediately.

Allowed to use the TX-0 whenever it was free, the hackers began to do amazing things. One programmed the machine to play Bach; another came up with software that would convert Arabic numerals to Roman numerals with lightning speed. (A faculty member, while he admired the feat, asked: "My God, why would anyone want to do such a thing?") Yet another hacker—a professor this time, rather than a student—created a prototypical computer game: A rectangular maze larded with wedge-shaped blips of light representing cheese was programmed to appear on the screen, and another blip, representing a mouse, moved through the maze in search of cheese. In a variation of the basic routine, the cheese wedges were replaced by martinis. As the mouse caroused from glass to glass, its movements grew increasingly erratic.

Soon another computer appeared at MIT. Dubbed the PDP-1—for Programmed Data Processor—the machine had been built by a new company founded by Kenneth Olsen, an MIT alumnus. After working on a major computer

Student members of the Tech Model Railroad Club at MIT look over a section of the club's elaborate setup in 1960. Many of the club members, fascinated by the intricate maze of electrical circuitry beneath the train layout, moved on to the even more intricate world of computers.

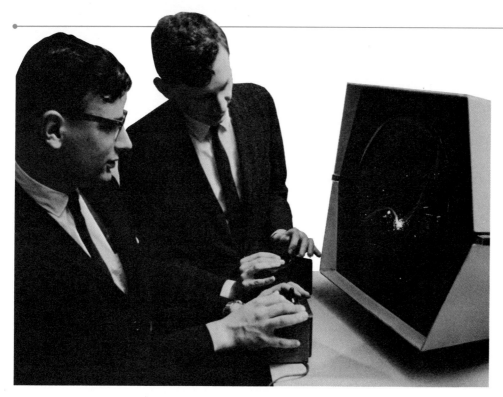

Nimble-fingered MIT computer enthusiasts of the early 1960s manipulate joysticks to play Spacewar! on the screen of a PDP-1 computer. Refining the software for this pioneering computer game introduced students to some of the more challenging aspects of programming.

project at his alma mater, Olsen had seen the need for a machine smaller than the huge mainframes of the day and had designed one himself. About the size of three refrigerators, priced at only a fraction of the cost of a conventional mainframe, this forerunner of the so-called minicomputers would in time revolutionize the entire computer industry. The MIT hackers loved it from the start.

One of the PDP-1's most intriguing tricks was devised by Marvin Minsky, a professor whose specialty was the infant field of artificial intelligence. Minsky wrote a program that generated three dots that worked together to create a variety of patterns—swirls, roses, geometric forms—on the machine's monitor screen.

Among the student hackers who were fascinated by this so-called Minskytron was Stephen Russell, a bespectacled young man with a passion for science fiction, bad movies and computers. Building on the Minskytron program, Russell indulged all three enthusiasms, working out a game in which two players could flip the PDP's toggle switches to maneuver a pair of missile-firing rocket ships— one slim and one chubby—on the machine's video screen. The object of the game was to blast the other player's ship out of the sky.

Russell called his rudimentary game Spacewar! He left copies of the program tape in a box near the PDP and invited fellow hackers to work out refinements to the program. They turned to the task with gusto. After a careful study of astronomical tables, one student wrote a routine that displayed the rocket ships against a background of the starry equatorial night sky; the game would move through 365 nights of stars every 24 hours. Another hacker made the gravitational pull of the sun and planets a force players had to take into account in plotting their maneuvers. Between forays for Chinese take-out food and Cokes—mainstays of the hacker diet—Russell and his friends played the game endlessly.

Spacewar! also generated a hardware spin-off. Finding it awkward to see the screen while controlling the rocket ships and missiles with switches on one side of the computer console, two of the regular players dreamed up another kind of device: They built what were probably the first computer joysticks—small wooden boxes with switches and buttons—so that space warriors could sit back or move around a bit instead of staying glued to the console.

Mouse-in-a-maze, Spacewar! and other games of the time—in fact, all of the hackers' programs—were in the public domain. Indeed, the hackers seemed to believe that the software they created should be freely available to other hackers everywhere—to anyone, in fact, with access to a computer. (Years later, hacker historian Steven Levy would name this philosophy the Hacker Ethic.) Copies of the programs—usually on paper tape that could be run directly on other PDPs or modified for different machines—circulated through an informal hacker network and found their way into the computer rooms of universities and corporations across the United States. The question of ownership did not arise, for these programs had no commercial value whatsoever at the time. Not until many more computers existed would this casual borrowing become an issue.

SOFTWARE GOES INDEPENDENT

In 1960, there were perhaps 5,000 computers in the United States. Those in commercial establishments were used most often for payroll, inventory control, invoicing, sales accounting and cost analysis. The military employed computers to operate air-defense and air-traffic-control systems.

At the time, most software was still being produced by the hardware manufacturers, who tailored programs to their own machines. But this situation was already showing signs of changing. A new kind of business operation appeared: the independent software vendor. One of the first such companies was started in the spring of 1959 by two young men from the aviation industry. Roy Nutt was a programmer at United Aircraft when he learned that another company needed a new compiler to translate a high-level programming language into machine code for their computer. He and his friend Fletcher Jones, an executive with North American Aviation, decided to bid on the job themselves. They got the bid, resigned their positions and formed—with $100 capital—Computer Sciences Corporation. Their new company grew at a dizzying pace: In 1964, CSC became the first software company listed on a national stock exchange.

For Nutt, Jones and other entrepreneurs in this fledgling industry, the principal customers initially were huge corporations or government agencies such as NASA. But the computer population was about to expand considerably, and with this growth would come a mushrooming demand for more diverse software.

The catalyst for this increase was none other than a cousin of the PDP-1, the machine on which Stephen Russell and his fellow hackers had honed the Spacewar! game. The PDP-8, the first commercially successful minicomputer, went on the market in 1965. Depending on its accessories and configuration, a PDP-8 could cost as little as $18,000—a price thousands of small engineering firms could afford. Machines made by other companies quickly followed it; by the end of the decade there were perhaps 100,000 computers in use worldwide.

No longer the province only of large and wealthy organizations, the computer began to inspire many new kinds of software, since the range of customers—from automobile dealerships to oil refineries—had an equally wide range of needs. Some software houses specialized in computer-aided design programs: Automobile manufacturers, architectural firms and aerospace projects all found the design process, from the drawing-board stage to tests for stress, more efficient with computerization. Geologists exploring for oil deposits armed themselves with computer-produced maps, and factories relied on minicomputers to guide robot arms assembling sections of automobiles.

Despite these developments, the next advance in hardware and software did not originate in the minicomputer industry, much less in the venerable mainframe establishment—or even in the software companies that had blossomed in the 1960s. With the invention of the microprocessor, the personal computer was born, and every hacker or hobbyist with a few hundred dollars could aspire to ownership of one. As a result of this tremendous broadening of computer usage, the Hacker Ethic came under severe strain.

A PAIR OF PROGRAMMING WIZARDS

The beginnings of the strain can be traced to the same 1975 *Popular Electronics* story on the Altair 8800 that had enthralled so many electronics and computer hobbyists. One of the most excited was Paul Allen, a young programmer who worked for Honeywell, a computer company near Boston. Allen immediately went to see his childhood friend William Gates, a Harvard freshman. The two young men decided that the little machine needed some software. And then, in a brash move that would live on in computer folklore, they made a phone call to the Altair's maker in Albuquerque. Gates and Allen spoke to MITS owner Ed Roberts. They had, they said, devised a program that translated BASIC into machine code for the Altair. Would Roberts be interested in buying it? Roberts replied that he would buy the first BASIC interpreter that he saw run in the Altair.

Gates and Allen worked feverishly to complete the program. As they did so, they drew heavily on their years of hacking together, which stretched back to their junior-high-school days in Seattle. The mothers' club of their school had bought the students time on a time-sharing system, and Gates taught himself how to program when he was just 13. While still in high school, the two boys formed a company they named Traf-O-Data; without much success, they tried to market computer analyses of traffic patterns to small towns in the Seattle area. But word of their programming skills spread, and a major software producer hired them to write programs for electric utilities in the Northwest and Canada. "No one knew then that we were just in ninth and 10th grades," Gates recalled later.

The experience served them well on the BASIC project, for they worked without ever having seen an Altair, much less used one. All they had to go on was an instructional manual for the Intel 8080 microchip employed in the machine. But that, combined with the Altair's specifications sheet, was enough for them to write a program simulating the new microcomputer's operation. They ran this on a larger computer to test their BASIC interpreter.

When they had their program in shape and punched out in final form on paper tape, Allen flew to Albuquerque to demonstrate it for Roberts—who had beefed up one of his Altairs with extra memory boards, a teletype and a tape reader. Only as his plane was about to land did Allen realize that he and Gates had forgotten to write the short but essential loader program—without which the Altair's microprocessor could not take in the BASIC program. Scribbling furiously, Allen dashed off the loader in machine language on a piece of scrap paper.

The next morning, Allen entered his last-minute addition, fed his BASIC tape into the machine and then crossed his fingers. After about five minutes, the program was loaded. Allen flipped the switches to run it, knowing full well that if he and Gates had made a mistake anywhere in the program, it would not work. And then, the Altair's teletype began to chatter. "MEMORY SIZE?" it typed.

Allen could breathe again. The program seemed to be working. He typed in a response: "7K." Then he entered an elementary problem: "PRINT 2 + 2." In a flash, the machine typed "4." As Bill Gates would remark later, Roberts and his MITS colleagues "got very excited. Nobody had ever seen the machine do anything." Roberts bought the program, and for the second time Allen and Gates formed a company, this one called Microsoft. They continued to refine the Altair BASIC interpreter and wrote other programs for the little machine. "It was pretty trashy stuff," Gates later said, "but people could have fun using the thing."

Few people were more fascinated by the Altair than the members of the recently formed Homebrew Computer Club, a loose conglomeration of computer enthusiasts in the Palo Alto, California, area. At their free-form meetings, club members exchanged information, technical tips, computer parts and programs. No piece of information about computer hardware or software, no matter how hard-earned, was withheld. The very essence of hackerdom, the Homebrewers coveted the Gates-Allen Altair BASIC. But MITS was selling the tape for $500, a sum that effectively put Altair BASIC out of reach of most Homebrewers.

In June of 1975, a group of MITS engineers staged an Altair seminar at a Palo Alto hotel. To the delight of the many Homebrew hackers who attended, the demonstration model Altair was running BASIC. The whole thing was just too tempting for one of the Homebrewers. He pocketed a spare tape that happened to be lying next to the Altair's chattering teletype. At the next meeting he asked a fellow club member to run off some copies. A tape soon was in the hands of every Homebrewer who wanted one; all a member had to do was make a couple of extra copies to hand on. In that fashion, Altair BASIC spread through the nation-wide hacker network to other clubs as well.

Having sold their program to MITS on a per-copy royalty basis, Allen and Gates were more than a little upset at this development. Their anger grew as it became clear that far fewer Altair users were buying their BASIC program than would have done so in the absence of the pirated version. After fuming for a time, Gates

Its front panel bristling with indicator lights and toggle switches, the Altair 8800 was a quaint machine in comparison with the sleek microcomputers of a later day. But the little Altair, which appeared in 1975, launched the personal computer boom.

Setting the Stage for a Video Game

Beneath the entertaining surface of a video game's sprightly graphics and lively sound effects lies a sophisticated computer program. To be successful, video game designers must not only possess the imagination and flair of a film maker, they must also be highly skilled programmers, able to tailor a game to computers with widely varying audio and video capabilities.

All video games are computer games, but not all computer games are video games. What distinguishes a video game from other computer recreations—fantasy adventures and word games, for example, or electronic versions of chess, poker and blackjack—is the visceral excitement generated by the video game's high-speed action and its constant demand for player response through a joystick or other control device. The player who hopes to do well must have quick reflexes and excellent hand-eye coordination. And the video game designer who hopes to score a hit with experienced players must find the right combination of variables to make a game fun and challenging.

The imaginary video game shown here and on the following pages serves to illustrate some of the basic elements of video game design. For example, the illusion of motion—the car racing around a corner, the train moving down the track—is achieved by changing the image on the screen several times each second. Part of the game designer's task is to pack the computer's memory with all the data necessary to create these rapid-fire images, then to write an efficient program that will assemble each new screenful of images a split second before revealing it to the player.

Creating a shape. Each shape that appears on the computer's screen begins as a simple image such as the silhouette of a car (top). The game designer then lays a grid over it (center) and squares the car's shape to create segments that can be encoded for storage in the computer's memory. Encoding the image involves assigning each filled square a one and each empty square a zero; in this simplified example, the result is a car formed of 16 rows of ones and zeros (bottom). The computer then draws the car by matching numbers with corresponding points on the screen, lighting up the ones and not the zeros. To draw a car in multiple colors, the computer would require more complex information—extra sets of numbers to tell the computer not only which points on the screen to light up but also what color they should be.

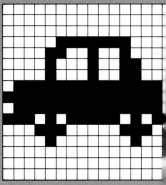

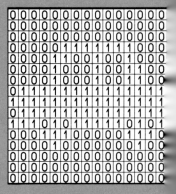

Making a shape table. Every figure in the game must be encoded and added to the video game's shape table, or catalogue of images, as a list of numbers. Figures such as the car and the jogger, both of which must appear to move, require several different entries in the shape table, one for each change in perspective or action. The shape table for this simple game would contain more than 100 shapes.

Constructing the set. One technique for making a video game run faster is to create a constant background so that the computer will not have to recalculate the position of each element every time it assembles a new screen. For an added touch of realism, the background shown here has one feature that is not constant: a ripple on the surface of the lake. The designer creates this effect by drawing several versions of the lake—one version with calm blue water, others with slightly different arrangements of white flecks on blue—and writing a loop in the program that tells the computer to interchange lake images at random during the game.

```
10   REM   EXPLOSION SUBROUTINE
20   FOR X = -10 TO 10
30        SOUND 0, 200, 4, 10-ABS(X)
40        SOUND 1, 255, 4, 10-ABS(X)
50        SOUND 2, 225, 4, 10-ABS(X)
60        SOUND 3, 150, 4, 10-ABS(X)
70   NEXT X
80   RETURN
```

CRASH

Creating a Library of Sounds

An important part of a video game's appeal is its sound effects; in the game shown on these pages, they might be noises such as train whistles, explosions and mooing. A computer produces sounds by sending electronic signals either to a built-in speaker or to an external unit connected to the machine. The designer tells the computer what signals to send by writing program routines that consist of batches of numbers that represent pitch, volume, distortion and other sound variables. Audio capabilities vary greatly among brands of computers, so the designer must find the desired sound effects for a given game by experimenting with the sounds available on the particular computer that will be used. The few lines of programming code displayed on the screen at left are part of a game program written in BASIC for an Atari home computer. With the right machine, these instructions would produce the explosive sound of a crash.

Human Reflexes versus Machine Logic

In the course of the road race game, the program's assembly of screen images and accompanying sound effects is governed by two factors—player input, or response, and the software's own internal logic. On each screen the program will renew constant landscape features, adjust joggers, cows and other figures whose movement is controlled by the software, and

With the joystick, the player controls the car's direction; pressing a trigger on the joystick causes the car to brake. The game software samples, or reads, signals from the joystick about 10 times per second and alters the car image on the screen accordingly. As the program assembles each new screen, it calculates whether the car has moved since the last screen, how far and in which direction it has moved, and whether it has collided with anything.

reposition the car on the basis of the player's most recent joystick signals. The program will also constantly update the player's elapsed time and follow built-in rules that dictate the consequences of collisions between the car and other figures on the screen.

Most video games include a variety of features designed to enliven play and challenge the player. This road race program, for example, adds interest with sound effects and animated graphics, and uses the two railroad crossings to incorporate an element of strategy into the race. A game designer might also throw in extra obstacles to increase the level of difficulty as the game continues.

The screen at left shows the driver 83 seconds into the race, on a collision course with an approaching train. The program generates a whistle and other danger signals—but what happens next depends on the player's reaction.

The scene below depicts what has happened one second (and perhaps eight screens) further into the game: The player did not brake in time, the race car crashed into the train and the program displays an explosion that ends the race with appropriate sound effects.

fired off an "Open Letter to Hobbyists." Appearing in several computer publications, the letter noted that while Gates and Allen had received many favorable comments about their program, most of those who praised it had not actually bought it. "Why is this?" Gates asked. He then answered his own question with a blunt accusation. "As the majority of hobbyists must be aware, most of you steal your software," Gates wrote. "Who can afford to do professional work for nothing?" he continued. "What hobbyist can put three man-years into programming, finding all the bugs, documenting his product and distributing it for free?"

To Gates the answer was obvious, but other people were not quite so sure. One recipient of Gates's letter, the editor of a small hobbyist publication, observed that "the most logical action was to tear the letter up and forget about it." And the members of at least one computer club talked of suing Gates for accusing them of thievery. Of the several hundred letters that Gates received in response to his complaint, many were negative, and only five or six included the voluntary payment that he had requested from users of contraband BASIC.

ENTER THE ENTREPRENEURS

The dispute between Gates and the hackers came to be known in computer circles as the software flap. Some hackers held to their ideals long after the flap had died down, writing and circulating so-called public domain programs for anyone who wanted them; these programs continue to be available on thousands of computer bulletin boards around the United States. But with the ranks of computer users growing at an extraordinary rate, Gates's viewpoint ultimately won out, for there was big money to be made in software.

One of the Homebrewers, Stephen Wozniak—a charter member of the club—played a key role in this alteration of the hardware and software landscape. In the spring of 1977, he and his friend and business partner Steven Jobs introduced their small, relatively inexpensive and fully assembled Apple II personal computer. Two other companies, Commodore and Radio Shack, already had similar machines on the market, but it was the Apple that touched off the personal computer explosion. Soon scores of competitors had entered the field, and millions of eager buyers rushed to obtain a personal computer of their own.

All of them needed software to make their machines useful, and there was no dearth of programmers and marketers ready to oblige them. Word-processing programs proved to be particularly popular—although, as is so often the case when it comes to innovation, the man who wrote the first such program for a microcomputer did not turn out to be the most successful entrant in the field.

In early 1975, Michael Shrayer, a New York film maker who had moved to California to find himself, joined the ranks of Altair kit buyers. Before long, he had beefed up his little machine with a keyboard and a television-screen monitor, and started selling some of the simple programs that he created for it. As his programs grew more complex, so did the manuals explaining how the programs functioned, and it occurred to Shrayer that it might be possible to do this manual writing on his Altair rather than on his typewriter. In explaining his motive, Shrayer later said: "To me, making things easier has always been the name of the game." He spent a year developing his program, working 16 to 20 hours a day. When he finished, he named the program Electric Pencil and began selling it.

Shrayer soon discovered that the potential market extended far beyond Altair

Sketches of Homebrew Computer Club members grace the cover of the group's second newsletter, dated April 12, 1975. Homebrewers, several of whom went on to become leaders in the software industry, formed their loose-knit group shortly after the introduction of the pathbreaking Altair personal computer.

owners. He wrote variations of Electric Pencil for other microcomputers and for a number of printers—78 versions in all. But this reprogramming was very time-consuming, as was the marketing of the product: Much of Shrayer's business was by mail, since there were fewer than 500 stores selling software at the time. For someone who was at heart a programmer and not a businessman, the pressures were unwelcome. In time, Shrayer lost interest, stopped promoting Electric Pencil and returned to full-time programming.

THE ADVENT OF INDUSTRY STANDARDS

For its first two years, Electric Pencil was virtually the only word-processing program available. But as the personal computer market became larger and more lucrative, other entrepreneurs followed Shrayer's lead. One was Seymour Rubinstein, a New Yorker who had started out as a programmer, and had worked as a systems consultant and a software buyer for a microcomputer manufacturer.

In 1978, Rubinstein became an independent software producer. Among the first people he hired was an ace programmer named John Barnaby. Rubinstein wanted one of his products to be a word processor, and he also wanted to make sure it would be well received in the marketplace. Before Barnaby had written a line, Rubinstein canvassed software dealers to find out what features they thought customers would favor. Then the two men tailored a program accordingly.

Rubinstein's planning paid off handsomely. The program they called WordStar took the market by storm, almost instantly becoming the standard for microcomputer word processing. According to some estimates, more microcomputer users processed words with WordStar over the next half-dozen years than with all other word-processing programs combined.

While Rubinstein was getting set to launch WordStar, Daniel Bricklin was attending classes at the Harvard Business School. An MIT graduate, Bricklin was a veteran of the computer industry. He had worked as a software engineer at Digital Equipment Corporation (DEC), builder of the PDP computer series, and had helped develop DEC's word-processing system before moving on to another company. His experience at both firms taught him that while he knew a lot about technology, he knew nothing of business, so he enrolled at Harvard.

In the course of his classwork, it occurred to Bricklin that there had to be a better way to perform the laborious calculations involved in such exercises as assessing the effect of an increase in interest rates on a company's costs and profits. The biggest problem was that each time one figure was changed, every figure derived from it had to be recomputed. An electronic calculator helped, but it was slow. And just one slip of the finger could botch the entire exercise, which was carried out on a large piece of elaborately ruled paper called a spreadsheet.

Bricklin's programming background led him to muse about turning this tedious number juggling over to a computer. He discussed his idea with his friend Robert Frankston, a freelance software engineer. Intrigued, Frankston started to work on a program in late 1978 and by the following spring had completed what he and Bricklin dubbed VisiCalc, short for Visible Calculator. On a personal computer's monitor screen, it generated columns of figures that would all change in an instant when one factor was altered. Using VisiCalc, corporate financial planners could, for example, make a swift, accurate estimate of the impact on their company's profits of a 6 per cent wage increase as opposed to a 7 per cent boost.

Bricklin and Frankston began marketing their program in the fall of 1979, and they were aided greatly by a plug from a financial analyst who called VisiCalc the "software tail that might wag the personal computer dog." This program, originally written for the Apple II, in fact played a key role in Apple's huge success. It was the first software package that would alone justify the purchase of a microcomputer system. In its first year on the market, as desktop-computer sales took off, VisiCalc was snapped up by 100,000 buyers, at approximately $200 a copy.

A perennial bestseller, VisiCalc spawned dozens of imitators eager to cash in on the same market. It also helped pave the way for other types of business software, not least among them dBASE II, a so-called data-base-management system that enabled computer users to file and organize large amounts of data, which could then be sorted and retrieved at will. The system was the creation of NASA engineer Wayne Ratliff, who developed the original program in his spare time and marketed it rather desultorily under the name Vulcan. It did not really take off until it came to the attention of software-marketing whiz George Tate.

A high-school dropout and Air Force veteran who in 1974 was working as a stereo repairman, Tate was one of the many eager buyers of the Altair computer

Entrepreneurs of the Software Revolution

In 1972, entrepreneur Nolan Bushnell installed the first of his coin-operated Pong games — video versions of Ping Pong — in a Sunnyvale, California, tavern. Not long afterward, the tavern owner informed Bushnell that the game was broken and suggested that he come and take it away. But when Bushnell investigated, he found that the machine was not broken at all. It had been stuffed so full of quarters that it was jammed.

That flood of quarters was the merest hint of what was to come. With a $500 investment, Bushnell started Atari. Four years later, he sold the company and pocketed $15 million; less than a decade after that, he reckoned his worth at $70 million.

As the microcomputer industry gained momentum in the 1970s and 1980s, a number of enterprising programmers, manufacturers and marketers joined Bushnell in hitting the financial jackpot. Shown here and on the following page is a sampling of some of the entrepreneurs who made it big.

1972
Nolan Bushnell of Atari launched the video game industry.

kit. When he finished assembling it, he found that the only thing he knew how to do was turn the machine on. "So I started at that point," he later recalled, "learning and understanding computers." Before long, he was so expert with the machine that he became a freelance computer repairman. In 1980, after a stint as western sales manager for a computer terminal company, Tate went into the software sales business with Hal Lashlee, a friend and fellow computer buff.

Tipped off to Ratliff's little-known Vulcan program, Tate and Lashlee negotiated a contract for exclusive distribution rights. Another company already had a claim on the Vulcan name, so the partners decided to call the product something else. Their advertising man came up with dBASE II. He thought it had a nice high-tech ring, and he also liked its none-too-subtle implication that the software was a newer—and presumably improved—version of a predecessor dBASE.

Of course, there had been no dBASE I to improve upon, but dBASE II was a dramatic improvement over other programs that sought to perform similar tasks. Introduced nationally with considerable hoopla in January 1981, the program quickly became a bestseller. Almost as quickly, Ratliff, Lashlee and Tate became the latest marchers in a growing parade of software millionaires.

1977
Steven Jobs *(left)* and Stephen Wozniak created the Apple computer.

75
Allen *(left)* and iam Gates ided Microsoft.

1976
Gary Kildall formed Digital Research Inc. to vend his CP/M operating system.

1979
Seymour Rubinstein *(right)* marketed WordStar, written by John Barnaby.

They were soon joined by yet another: Mitchell Kapor, whose wildly successful Lotus 1-2-3 program combined some of the best features of VisiCalc's spreadsheet with graphics and information-retrieval capabilities. Like many of the young men who hit it big in the glory days of the personal computer software game, Kapor seemed an unlikely recruit to the ranks of the rich. Raised on Long Island, he was a whiz in mathematics and racked up an impressive high-school record. But at Yale, where he majored in psychology and linguistics, his grades were only average—possibly because he spent too much time at the campus radio station, where he eventually became music director; he also took up Transcendental Meditation, pursuing it seriously enough to qualify as an instructor.

After graduation from Yale in 1971, Kapor spent two years as a disc jockey, then moved to Cambridge, Massachusetts, and went to work as a computer programmer. "My job was incredibly boring," he would recall later. By 1975, he had quit and turned to teaching meditation full-time, first in Cambridge, then at the exotic Maharishi International University in Iowa. Seeking something more—he was not quite sure what—he flew to Switzerland for a concentrated six-month course in meditation. There, he said, "I was locked up in a hostel with

1981
George Tate (right) marketed dBASE II, developed by Wayne Ratliff.

1979
Daniel Bricklin (background) and Robert Frankston launched VisiCalc.

1982
Mitchell Kapor introduced Lotus 1-2-3 with a million-dollar ad campaign.

100 born-again Hindus and got into the habit of crying a lot." Tiring of that regimen, he returned to Cambridge and went into psychotherapy.

And then, in 1978, he started fiddling around with personal computers, trading in his elaborate stereo system for an Apple II. Kapor was soon a dedicated programmer, and eventually worked up two promising business programs that he marketed through the same company that had made such a hit of VisiCalc. Before long, Kapor's royalty checks started to run into the six-figure range. Unsatisfied, he sold all his rights to the two programs for $1.2 million and went on to establish a company to make and market his multipurpose Lotus 1-2-3.

Kapor had timed his new venture well. In August 1981, IBM officially confirmed its long-rumored entry into the personal computer market, unveiling the new IBM PC. Kapor designed Lotus 1-2-3 to work on IBM's 16-bit processor rather than on the eight-bit processor characteristic of the other microcomputers then available. He reasoned that IBM's preeminence would soon make this processor the standard throughout the personal computer industry, giving his program a jump on the competition. Kapor's surmise was right on the mark: Introduced in late 1982 with a million-dollar national advertising campaign, Lotus 1-2-3 quickly soared to the top of software's bestseller chart. By July, 60,000 customers had shelled out $495 each for their copies of the program.

Kapor's new company rode to riches on IBM's billowing coattails, as did many another software maker that designed its programs to run on the IBM PC—and on the spate of copycat machines that other manufacturers began to churn out. IBM's entry into the field was a watershed event. Not only did IBM itself sell large numbers of machines, but the huge and long-established company's mere presence in the market convinced many dubious consumers that personal computers—no matter who made them—were worthy of serious attention.

Another effect of IBM's arrival was a wholesale switch among microcomputer manufacturers from one operating system to another. An operating system is the unglamorous but essential software that coordinates the internal workings of the machine. It acts as a sort of orchestra leader to ensure that the computer's complex hardware works harmoniously with the applications software to accomplish what the user has instructed the machine to do. Programs written for one operating system cannot work on another system, so the supplier of an operating system that becomes an industry standard can count on bountiful profits.

Most of the eight-bit machines that dominated the industry before IBM's entry used an operating system called CP/M, for Control Program for Microcomputers. The system had been devised in 1974 by computer scientist Gary Kildall, and it came into its own two years later, after the Altair had kicked off the microcomputer boom. At the same time, as more and more computer makers built their machines to run on CP/M, the system became the standard for software designers. Then IBM decided to get into the picture.

According to software-industry folklore—and for such a young industry, software is heavy with folklore—Kildall was putting his private aircraft through its paces when a pair of IBM officials came calling to discuss an operating system for their proposed personal computer. Entranced by the freedom of the skies, and ever-disdainful of corporate niceties, the quirky Kildall declined to come down to earth and talk business. Or so the story goes.

According to Kildall, he discussed the matter briefly and inconclusively with

IBM but then flew off on a two-week vacation in the Caribbean. By the time he got back, IBM had hammered out a deal with another company: the same Microsoft headed by the same Bill Gates who had programmed the pioneer Altair in 1975. Christened MS-DOS (for Microsoft Disk Operating System) and blessed by IBM, the new system was adopted by the scores of computer makers who rushed into the arena with machines that were compatible with the IBM PC. Gates's MS-DOS had usurped the place of Kildall's CP/M—and in a greatly expanded market.

By the mid-1980s, the software boom seemed to have leveled off. Yesterday's shaggy hacker-programmer had cleaned up and put on a suit and tie. Many of the companies that had started out with a few hundred or a few thousand dollars in capital had gone public and become major corporations. Market-research techniques had become a standard part of the developmental process for software; advertising budgets grew into the millions for a single new-product launch. The scale and cost of doing business made it increasingly difficult for newer companies or individuals with a good product to move into a competitive position.

And yet, something of the old hacker spirit still remained, for at the heart of the software business is a creative process that is inherently difficult, if not impossible, to control: programming. Paul Lutus, a particularly imaginative programmer and the creator of numerous top-selling software products for Apple computers, is not wholly atypical. Lutus, who for a long time labored in the splendid isolation of a mountaintop cabin that he built with his own hands, refuses to work on anybody else's projects. "If I didn't have the idea myself," he explains, "I would be bored with it and I wouldn't do a very good job."

As one industry observer has remarked, "the programmer's muse is an untamed one. Great software, like great writing, adheres to no known schedule of production." And the next VisiCalc, WordStar or Lotus 1-2-3 is as likely to come from someone like Paul Lutus as from a corporate research department.

Working in this rustic 12-by-16-foot Oregon cabin, the fiercely independent Paul Lutus wrote the best-selling Apple Writer word-processing program, published in 1979. A few years later, the program was yielding its creator more than $7,500 per day in royalty payments.

Four Lightning Laborers

The software industry has spawned tens of thousands of programs for personal computers, an outpouring as diverse as the interests of the growing population of computer users. There are programs to write astrological charts, to keep track of a restaurant's wine inventory, to help doctors diagnose disease, to create business-oriented graphics, to teach French or calculus or even computer programming. Moreover, these various kinds of software resemble one another scarcely at all. Between the explosive sound effects of a galactic war game and the discreet beeps of an accounting package, the gulf is so wide that no common features are apparent. Yet despite their outward diversity, all programs—even those for giant mainframes—must perform some of the same basic functions. For example, although the details vary, all programs must store information in temporary memory, remember where it is located and retrieve it in a particular way in order to carry out their functions.

Among the most important functions are text manipulation, calculation, organization of information, and the management of input and output. Some of these functions are immediately evident in every program; translating signals from the keyboard into images on the screen is one kind of input/output management, for example. Others—such as the calculations required to plot the paths of race cars in a game program—are barely discernible as they do their work. Usually the functions are so intertwined that it is hard to say where one ends and another begins.

Although most of the functions operate to some degree in every program, one sometimes predominates. Calculations, for example, are the underpinnings of a financial spreadsheet, and input/output management figures large in a graphics program that turns signals from a device such as a light pen into spectacular displays on the screen. The illustrations on the following pages are designed to demonstrate how certain fundamental program types use specific software techniques to manipulate information to produce the desired results.

Putting Words in the Proper Place

The English poet Samuel Taylor Coleridge summarized his craft as the art of putting "the best words in their best order." Down through the ages, writers of all kinds have struggled to achieve that deceptively simple goal, laboriously making new drafts and generating wastebaskets full of rejects.

A computer with word-processing software drastically alters this procedure, allowing the writer to make all changes on an electronic copy of the document — a copy that exists only in the computer's malleable memory. Deleting and inserting words, checking spelling, moving whole paragraphs, even finding and replacing a specified word throughout a document can all be accomplished with a few keystrokes. Thus the first version to appear on paper can be a clean, error-free document — whether or not it qualifies as poetry.

A trick of memory. Word-processing software stores each character, space (▲) and carriage return (⏎) of a document in one byte of memory and records its location. When the document is edited, the program changes the order in which it reads the symbols; here, the program stores an inserted word — "half" — out of order in memory, but reads and displays it in the correct order, after "cancel" (opposite).

Editing: The old way
An intermediate draft of a hand-written document shows the signs of a writer's handiwork — special marks that indicate changes to be made when the next copy is typed out.

Editing: The new way

INSERT

With a word processor, the writer adds a word ("half") by moving the pointer, or cursor, to the right place, entering the INSERT command and typing the new word. The program automatically shifts the rest of the sentence to the right.

DELETE

To delete a block of text, the writer marks its beginning and end, then enters the DELETE command. The program removes the words from the screen and moves the text left to fill the gap.

BLOCK MOVE

To move a block of text, the writer marks it, positions the cursor at the insertion point and enters the MOVE command. The program removes the block from the screen, then reorders the sequence of words it reads out of memory to show the text in its new position.

FORMAT

Once the writer has made all the changes, special format commands can change the look of a document on the page. Thus, the first paper copy can be the clean final draft.

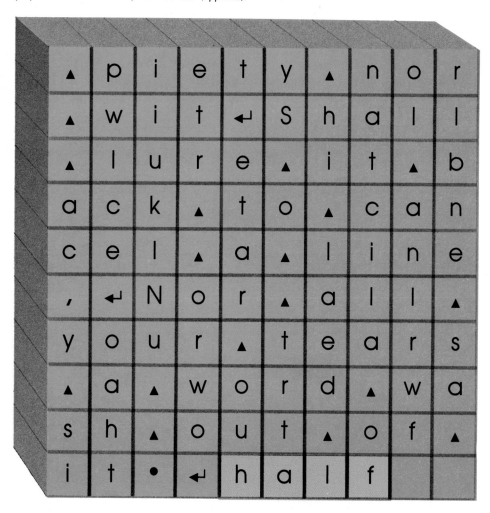

The moving finger writes; and, having writ,
Moves on to the next thing: Nor all your piety nor wit
Shall lure it back to cancel half a line,
Nor all your tears [a word] [wash out] of it

The moving finger writes; and, having writ,
Moves on to the next thing: nor all your piety nor wit
Shall lure it back to cancel half a line,
Nor all your tears a word wash out of it.

The moving finger writes; and, having writ,
Moves on to the next thing: nor all your piety nor wit
Shall lure it back to cancel half a line,
Nor all your tears a word wash out of it.

The moving finger writes; and, having writ,
Moves on: nor all your piety nor wit
Shall lure it back to cancel half a line,
Nor all your tears a word wash out of it.

The moving finger writes; and, having writ,
Moves on: nor all your piety nor wit
Shall lure it back to cancel half a line,
Nor all your tears wash out a word of it.

Fast Work with Numbers and Formulas

At the core of a spreadsheet program lies the computer's greatest strength: the ability to manipulate numbers and complex formulas with enormous speed and flexibility. Modeled after the traditional work sheets used by accountants, an electronic spreadsheet is divided by rows and columns into hundreds or even thousands of individual cells. Although only a few of these cells are visible on the screen at any one time, it is possible to shift the viewing window rapidly from point to point on the sheet with a few simple commands. Once the user has entered labels, numbers or formulas into the cells, the computer can calculate and display results almost instantaneously. And if the contents of any one cell are changed, the program allows for the instant recalculation of all relevant figures in the entire sheet.

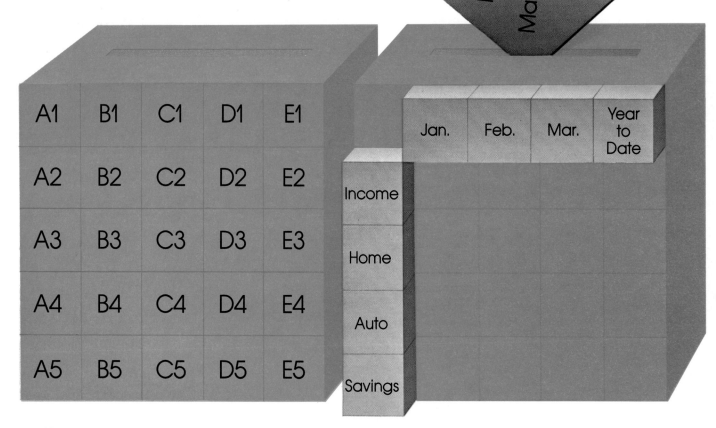

A grid for custom calculations
A spreadsheet first appears on the screen as an array of empty cells, each identified by the coordinates of its column and row (letters and numbers, respectively, in the example above). Whenever the program refers to the contents of a cell, it is by these coordinates; all operations are thus independent of the specific values entered in the cells.

Labels to clarify the structure
Labels in cells at the head of the columns and rows act as reminders of the relationships among the elements of the spreadsheet. In the example above, the labels define a spreadsheet to keep track of monthly and year-to-date totals of family income and expenses.

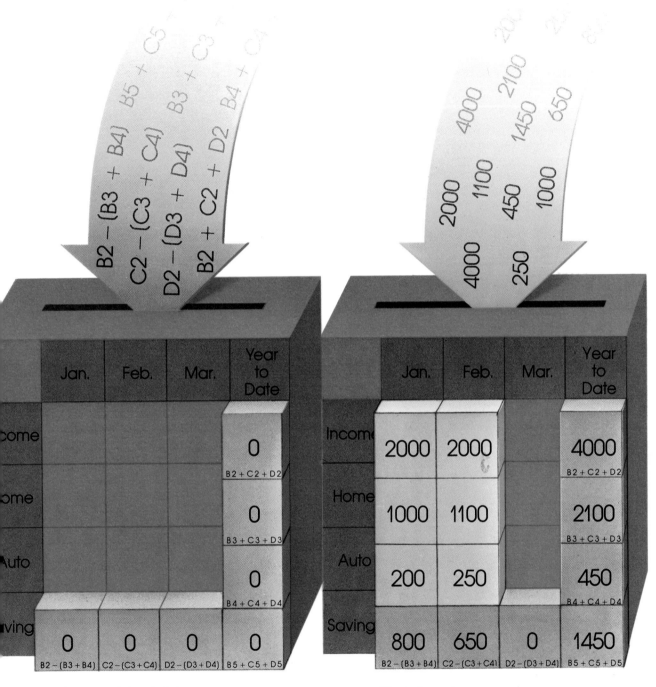

	Jan.	Feb.	Mar.	Year to Date
come				0
				B2 + C2 + D2
ome				0
				B3 + C3 + D3
Auto				0
				B4 + C4 + D4
ving	0	0	0	0
	B2 – (B3 + B4)	C2 – (C3 + C4)	D2 – (D3 + D4)	B5 + C5 + D5

	Jan.	Feb.	Mar.	Year to Date
Incom	2000	2000		4000
				B2 + C2 + D2
Home	1000	1100		2100
				B3 + C3 + D3
Auto	200	250		450
				B4 + C4 + D4
Saving	800	650	0	1450
	B2 – (B3 + B4)	C2 – (C3 + C4)	D2 – (D3 + D4)	B5 + C5 + D5

Formulas to control the calculations
A formula in a cell requires the program to display in that cell the results of the calculations described by the formula. Each formula is a combination of mathematical functions and the cell coordinates of the data to be used in the computation. When no values are entered in the relevant cells, the formula generates a zero.

Filling in the numbers
Plugging values into cells in the spreadsheet causes an instantaneous reaction: The program updates every cell containing a formula that refers to the coordinates of cells holding new data. If cells referred to by the formula contain no numbers, then zeros appear.

Organizing and Managing Information

Record keeping has been a hallmark of civilization since the days of clay tablets and papyrus scrolls. Stories about chaotic filing systems probably began with the first tax rolls of antiquity, and they persist in the bureaucracies of modern corporations and governments. Records must be well organized to be useful, but even the most sophisticated paper filing system has inherent limitations.

For example, a magazine publisher might keep a subscriber card file, each card containing the name and address of the subscriber, and the date the subscription expires. If the file is arranged so that the names are in alphabetical order, it will be easy to find an individual card when a subscriber submits a change of address. But when the publisher needs to know which subscriptions run out in a given month, the best arrangement for the cards is chronological, by expiration date. And to analyze the geographic distribution of subscribers, the cards would need to be arranged by city or state. Unless there were three separate files, each job would require leafing through the file, card by card, to find the required information.

Data-base-management programs eliminate this inefficiency. Information need be entered only once, in a kind of master file. When the program is instructed to sort the data or to compile a list, it can search rapidly through the information in memory (or on a storage disk or tape), copying any part of the data into a new file with a different order — all without changing the original set of information in any way.

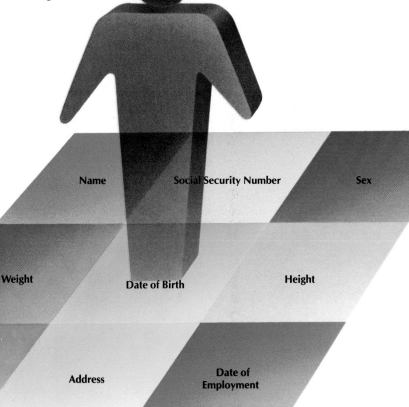

Data-base-management software organizes information into files containing individual records. A record, represented here by the large square, is made up of separate items of information called fields, represented by the small colored squares. In a personnel file, as in this example, designated fields might include name, date of birth and occupation. Specific information would vary, of course, but each record would contain the same designated fields.

Name   Social Security Number   Sex

Weight   Date of Birth   Height

Occupation   Address   Date of Employment

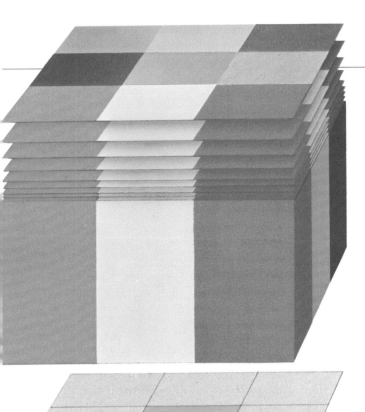

Scanning a file electronically
The program can quickly scan an entire file, looking at only one field in each record, and then take further action based on what it finds. Two common options are searching, or identifying all records with the same information in a given field, and sorting, or arranging records in a specified way, such as in alphabetical or numerical order.

Date of Birth

Sex

Occupation   Address   Date of Employment

Occupation   Date of Employment

Occupation   Date of Employment

Searching for a common attribute
In the simplest kind of search, the program examines one field in each record, looking for a specified attribute. In this example, the problem is to find all employees who are 25 years old. The program examines the date-of-birth field *(green)* of each record in the personnel file. Only if this field contains the specified year of birth does the program identify the record as meeting the search criterion.

Searching for a combination of attributes
A more complex search can refer to more than one field. In this example, the problem is to identify all female attorneys with more than five years' employment who live within a particular area. Using occupation *(blue)* as the first field, the program checks a record to see whether the employee is an attorney. If this is the case, the program next checks the sex and date-of-employment fields *(purple and pink)*. If these fields also contain the specified values, the program goes on to the last field, address *(yellow)*. If this field indicates the correct zip code, the program identifies the record as meeting the criteria.

Searching for more than one combination
A search can also look for more than one combination of attributes. In this example, the problem is to identify all clerks with more than five years' employment and all messengers with less than two years' employment. If the occupation field holds either clerk or messenger, the program looks in the date-of-employment field. If this field contains one of the specified dates — less than two years ago for messengers or more than five years ago for clerks — the program identifies the record as meeting the criteria.

Graphic Prestidigitation

Part of every computer program is devoted to interpreting incoming information, or input, and to presenting processed results in a useful form, or output. Most computers have hardware that lets them receive input from a keyboard and send output to a monitor or printer. Specialized software opens the door to more diverse applications.

Many of these applications require additional hardware designed for particular input or output functions. Input devices range from the graphics tablets used by artists (opposite) to equipment that can interpret voice commands, or sense changes in temperature or atmospheric pressure. While output can be displayed in many forms on a printer or a video monitor (below), there are also specialized output devices such as process controllers that govern traffic lights or machine tools, and audio synthesizers, which simulate musical instruments or human voices. Software tells the computer how to use these devices to get the desired results.

Graphics software allows a designer to use a computer to produce a dazzling array of images. But each simple command, each change of the image on the monitor, requires an enormous amount of computation — with every unseen step controlled by the program.

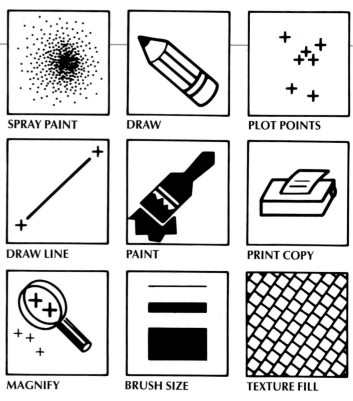

SPRAY PAINT   DRAW   PLOT POINTS

DRAW LINE   PAINT   PRINT COPY

MAGNIFY   BRUSH SIZE   TEXTURE FILL

The power of a graphics program derives from the program's ability to translate a simple input command into the computations that result in a complex output to the screen. Often these commands are invoked through icons — symbols of the graphic effects they represent — like those shown here. Icons may be designated keys on a keyboard, or the software may display them on the monitor, to be selected by positioning the cursor and pressing a special key or button.

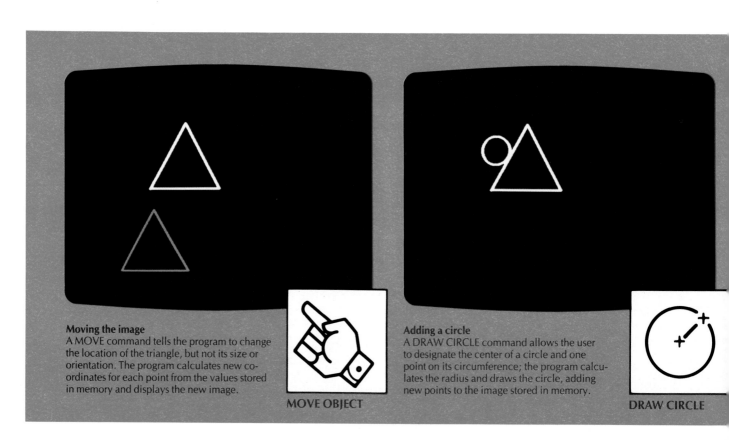

Moving the image
A MOVE command tells the program to change the location of the triangle, but not its size or orientation. The program calculates new coordinates for each point from the values stored in memory and displays the new image.

MOVE OBJECT

Adding a circle
A DRAW CIRCLE command allows the user to designate the center of a circle and one point on its circumference; the program calculates the radius and draws the circle, adding new points to the image stored in memory.

DRAW CIRCLE

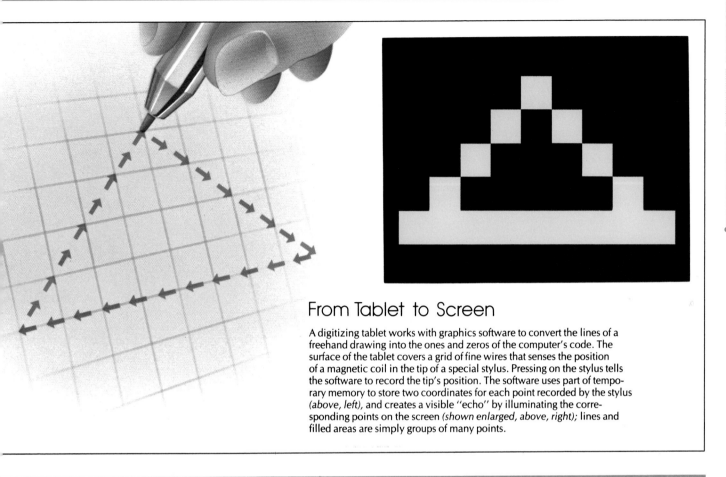

From Tablet to Screen

A digitizing tablet works with graphics software to convert the lines of a freehand drawing into the ones and zeros of the computer's code. The surface of the tablet covers a grid of fine wires that senses the position of a magnetic coil in the tip of a special stylus. Pressing on the stylus tells the software to record the tip's position. The software uses part of temporary memory to store two coordinates for each point recorded by the stylus *(above, left)*, and creates a visible "echo" by illuminating the corresponding points on the screen *(shown enlarged, above, right)*; lines and filled areas are simply groups of many points.

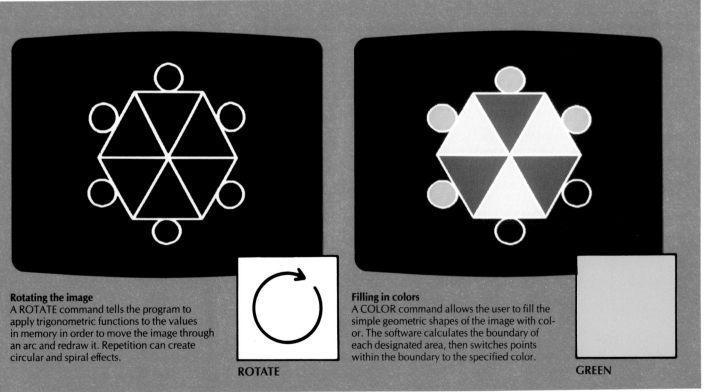

Rotating the image
A ROTATE command tells the program to apply trigonometric functions to the values in memory in order to move the image through an arc and redraw it. Repetition can create circular and spiral effects.

ROTATE

Filling in colors
A COLOR command allows the user to fill the simple geometric shapes of the image with color. The software calculates the boundary of each designated area, then switches points within the boundary to the specified color.

GREEN

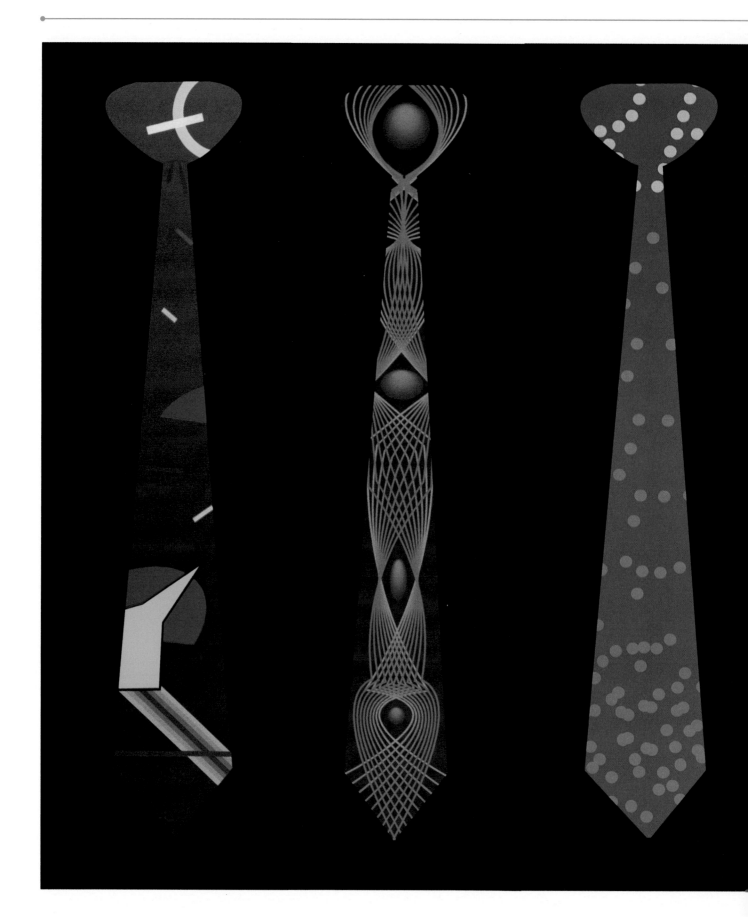

A Quantum Leap in Control

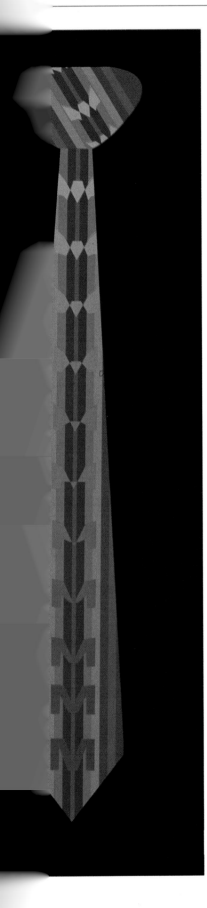

When Henry Barnes took the job as Denver's traffic engineer in late 1947, he knew right away that he had a problem. Like many other urban areas, the Mile-High City was faced with ever-increasing congestion as commuter traffic thronged the central city. By instituting one-way streets and installing hundreds of new traffic lights, Barnes improved the situation somewhat, but it soon became clear that these conventional remedies could not provide a real solution.

Barnes, a former electrician who had educated himself with 20 years of night school courses, was a colorful man in a gray line of work. Called "Hustling Hank" because of his restless energy, the cigar-puffing traffic chief spent part of his 60-hour weeks driving through the streets of Denver looking for traffic snarls. Most of these missions were observational, but sometimes he took direct action. On one foray he came upon a broken signal controller that was keeping 59 downtown traffic lights from changing. Barnes worked the timer manually for an hour and a half until a replacement part arrived. The incident convinced him that Denver's antiquated traffic control system needed to be thoroughly revised.

What Barnes wanted was equipment that could respond to changing situations, controlling traffic flow throughout the downtown area by adjusting the timing of all the lights. No such system existed, so he undertook to design one himself. On a trip to New York to meet with traffic device manufacturers, he sketched the outline of his idea on a hotel tablecloth for two electronics engineers. Two years of development followed. In 1952 the equipment was installed at a cost of $115,000—nearly 17 times Denver's total traffic budget for 1948.

At the heart of the system was an electromechanical controller that Barnes's staff referred to as "the Thing." A composite of vacuum tubes, timers, motors and dials strung together by five miles of wire, it reacted mechanically to external events. Cars driving through downtown Denver passed over pressure-sensitive devices, which forwarded signals to the controller. Every six minutes, the Thing tallied the number of signals received from each sensor, determining the volume of traffic moving in each direction. It used this information to change the timing of lights at 110 intersections, gradually lengthening the green period for streets with heavy traffic, shortening it for more lightly traveled routes.

In 1953, Denver's evening rush hour routinely ended 20 minutes earlier than it had in 1947, and traffic fatalities were reduced by almost half, even though the number of cars in the city had increased by 44 per cent. Other cities, their streets choked by similar increases in auto traffic, began to turn to electronic solutions; by the mid-1960s, more than 100 cities around the world had adopted systems similar to the one in Denver. In the years that followed, the nation's automobile population continued its rapid growth, and general-purpose computers with traffic control software began to replace specialized machines like the Thing. By the 1980s, computerized traffic control had become the main bulwark against total paralysis in many cities.

Denver's traffic management equipment was a precursor of process control systems that would appear in such diverse places as factory production lines, nuclear power plants and banks of automatic elevators. A process control system is a combination of computers, software and mechanical devices that interacts mainly with the physical world, not with a human operator, at a pace dictated by external events. Process control systems are widely used because they can respond consistently to huge volumes of input.

But process control is only one area where the speed and accuracy of computers have been applied to the increasingly complex problems of a modern society. As general-purpose computers became more available during the 1960s and 1970s, they were programmed to do a multitude of tasks. Businesses from banks and airlines to baseball teams developed software to help them cope with mountains of information that would have required prohibitive outlays of time and money if handled by human beings. At first, many of these applications used batch processing, entering transactions in batches some time after they occurred. But in some industries, the need to maintain accurate up-to-the-minute information is critical. The solution is a computer system and software that allow many users to read and alter the contents of a large data base as their work requires. Changes made by any user are entered into the data base and are immediately available to all users. This kind of operation is called on-line transaction processing because users can enter their transactions through a live, or on-line, connection rather than through the delayed action of batch processing.

AUTOMATING AIR TRAVEL

Airlines in the United States, expanding rapidly in the 1950s, pioneered on-line transaction-processing systems to keep close track of the availability of seats on their flights. To operate efficiently, airlines need to fill as many seats as possible on each flight and yet avoid overbooking, which could result in lost business from inconvenienced passengers. Developing a seat reservation system was a daunting prospect, since a single airline might have thousands of seats each day on flights to many destinations, and hundreds of reservation agents continually accepting reservation inquiries and cancellations from prospective passengers. An effective system would have to be accessible at all times, consistently provide fast, accurate responses and be easy for reservation agents to learn quickly.

Throughout the 1950s, airlines and computer companies struggled to develop suitable machines and software. Some early systems were partial measures: At best, they could indicate whether or not a flight was sold out. For example, Trans World Airlines in 1958 installed terminals for reservation agents in six cities, with the demand for seats being collated by computers at three separate sites. These computers reported each sale or cancellation by teletype to a central inventory, where control agents kept records of available seats. The control agents notified the computers, also by teletype, when a flight was fully booked; the information was relayed electronically to the reservation agents' terminals.

A better approach was already on the way. IBM, working at first with American Airlines and later with Pan American and Delta, developed a reservation system that revolutionized the air-travel industry; its hardware and software features came to be incorporated into systems used by more than 20 other airlines. The system, now called SABRE (for Semi-Automatic Business Research Environment), took eight years to design and install. When the pioneer version went into service for American Airlines in 1964, it comprised a transcontinental network of 2,000 terminals linked to a large central computer. At the time it was the world's largest commercial application of real-time, or immediate, processing.

The essential job of SABRE was to provide a central data base accessible to each reservation agent, anywhere in the system; the data base would be updated as soon as an agent sold, changed or cancelled a ticket on any flight segment in the system. Agents would be able to conduct an entire reservation transaction in one phone call, and be sure that the information they were getting from the computer was accurate and current to the moment.

The software also had to control the communications network and the central computer. Each terminal sent its messages over cable lines to a local concentrator. This electronic storage device held messages from several agents until software controlling the central computer polled each concentrator in turn, instructing it to send along whatever messages had accumulated in the second or two since the last polling cycle. The job was handled so smoothly and swiftly that the effect was the same as having a computer that served each individual terminal.

A VALUABLE VERSATILITY

From the start, SABRE did more than provide quick service to passengers. It was capable of maintaining a record of passenger reservations—a vast improvement over simple seat inventories. SABRE also provided American with a huge, readily accessible data base—a tool for increasing control over daily operations and for developing long-term plans. SABRE and its descendants soon became indispensable, handling loads that would be impossible for a human network; by the late 1980s, some individual airline systems incorporated more than 100,000 terminals, with the central computer handling as many as 2,000 messages per second. Seat reservation is only one of the functions the airlines' systems have come to serve. Agents can issue tickets and boarding passes, assign seats, order special meals, book hotel rooms, arrange limousine service, and provide translators, secretaries and baby-sitters. The systems are also used to track cargo and baggage, check credit, send electronic messages and purchase foreign currency.

The lessons learned in developing seat reservation systems proved valuable in a wide range of transaction-processing applications. SABRE was one of the first commercial applications of computer time sharing. For SABRE, time sharing was a relatively straightforward operation, since all users were running the same type of program. In other situations, such as a university—where one user might be running a program to analyze economic data while another processed the results of an experiment in organic chemistry—time sharing was much harder to implement. For example, the software not only had to be able to allocate memory space, processing time and resources such as tape or disk drives, it also had to prevent users from inadvertently destroying one another's data or programs. IBM spent millions of dollars and struggled for years during the 1960s to match time-sharing software with its newest, most powerful computers; estimates of programming costs ballooned from eight million dollars in 1961 to $44.5 million in 1966. One of the supervisors of the project noted that IBM learned many technical concepts from the work, but that "it was a very expensive education."

More immediately successful for IBM was the software it developed for handling many messages at once and harnessing several central processors to speed up the SABRE system's performance. The operating system that made this possible was originally called the Airline Control Program (ACP); later known as TPF, for Transaction Processing Facility, it was used for high-capacity real-time systems in a number of other industries. One of those industries was banking.

Thousands of times each day, at city street corners and shopping malls all across the United States, people step up to computer terminals called ATMs (automatic teller machines) and use plastic cards to do their banking without going into a bank. Usually, ATMs are connected to the bank's main computer. There, a program processes transactions immediately, sending the appropriate messages to the customer through the ATM. Cash deposits and withdrawals, account transfers and even bill payments are performed instantaneously; the machine issues a receipt to the customer, and the program updates the bank's central files. Tellers in the bank branches have access to those same central files to check or change critical information about accounts.

But this kind of on-line data processing is a recent development. Bankers first looked to computers to save them from an approaching tidal wave of paper. The number of checks handled in the United States swelled from 5.3 billion in 1945 to 9.5 billion in 1955. Recording and processing these checks and the multitude of papers involved in loans and other financial activities required huge amounts of hand-sorting by bank clerks; prospective growth threatened to swamp them.

IN SEARCH OF A SOLUTION
Early in the 1950s, the San Francisco-based Bank of America, then the world's largest retail bank, handling twice as much paper as any other, acted to avert the crisis. At that time, checking accounts were not numbered, and few bank customers used checks printed with their name and address. Clerks had to decipher the signatures, sort the checks alphabetically, then finally post them, by name, to the customer's account. Faced with an ever-growing load, Bank of America turned to the nearby Stanford Research Institute, now known as SRI International, for help.

The solutions that resulted were so successful that they became industry standards. The first was an entire system for numbering and reading checks, called magnetic ink character recognition (MICR). The system used special scanners to read numbers printed with magnetic ink on each check; the numbers identified the bank's location, name and branch, and the individual account number. Easy enough for humans to read, the numbers had the advantage of being readable by machines even when they were covered with the multiple endorsement stamps most checks received in their passage from bank to bank.

The second of SRI's solutions was a bookkeeping system called ERMA, for Electronic Recording Method of Accounting. In addition to using MICR scanners, ERMA employed a computer designed by SRI and built by General Electric, with software created by the bank. In 1959 Bank of America began to install the first of 32 ERMA systems in its regional centers around California.

Eventually, computers took over much of the day-to-day drudgery of the banking business. During the 1960s and 1970s, as computer costs went down and banks' clerical burdens went up, overnight batch processing of the day's transactions became common practice at many banks. Then terminals were provided to tellers, who could call up critical account information from on-line data bases. As the systems that did this work became more sophisticated, bankers came to see advantages in using the technology to attract customers. Automatic teller machines began to appear in the early 1970s. Although initial customer reaction was lukewarm, banks continued to push the machines when it became clear that they were an effective way to reduce the high cost of using human tellers to conduct simple transactions. And as ATMs became more reliable and easier to use, customer acceptance grew; in the late 1970s one New York bank reported that more than two thirds of all cash withdrawals were made at machines, and many customers chose to use ATMs even when human tellers were available. Twenty years of hardware and software development had turned bank computers from backroom number crunchers into helpers for ordinary people.

A NATIONWIDE NETWORK

While the value of many early computer applications was counted in dollars and cents, one system was measured by a different standard—human lives saved. It is an axiom of working with machinery that safety rules are written in blood; too often, new procedures are instituted only after a serious accident. A tragic case in point is the automation of the U.S. air-traffic-control (ATC) system. Prior to 1956, the idea of automating air-traffic control had received only desultory attention. But in that year, a devastating midair collision brought the issue to center stage.

In the mid-1950s, aircraft were directed by controllers only on takeoff and landing. Airliners' locations were plotted by hand and based on estimates called in by the pilots. There was no sophisticated long-range radar system, and there were no computers.

On June 30, 1956, a Saturday morning, something happened to change all that. Shortly after 9 o'clock, two airplanes cleared the runway at Los Angeles airport within minutes of each other, climbing out of the overcast above the airport into sunlit skies. Trans World Airlines Flight 2, a Lockheed Super Constellation heading for Kansas City, leveled off at 19,000 feet. United Airlines Flight 718, a Douglas DC-7 bound for Chicago, did the same at 21,000 feet. Then the Constellation changed its flight plan and got clearance to go to 21,000 feet.

As was the custom, the pilots of the two planes periodically called in to the nearest air-control terminal to report their positions and estimated times of arrival over various designated points on the ground along their routes. These advisory reports were relayed by phone to the next regional control station, where they were printed on long pieces of paper called flight-progress strips; controllers monitoring the flights sat in front of tall racks that could hold 20 or more strips. This information was intended only to keep the controller posted as to the progress of the flights. Once the two planes left the Los Angeles terminal area, however, they were in uncontrolled airspace. Neither plane was being directed from the ground, and neither was aware of the other's presence. But by 10:13 the Salt Lake City control center had received reports from both planes; each expected to pass over the Painted Desert checkpoint at 10:31.

A FINAL MESSAGE

Meanwhile, weather conditions had changed. Scattered clouds at 15,000 feet turned into a solid cloud layer, with thunderheads in places rising to 25,000 feet. To avoid severe turbulence, pilots usually flew around thunderheads rather than through them. Exactly what happened will never be known, but at precisely 10:31, the Super Constellation and the DC-7 collided in midair over the Painted Desert. At that moment, Salt Lake City control received a single radio transmission: "Salt Lake, United 718 . . . ah . . . we're going in." Nothing else was heard from either plane; all 117 passengers and 11 crew members were killed as the mutilated airliners fell into the Grand Canyon below.

The horror of the seemingly preventable accident set off a public and political furor that led directly to major reforms in civilian air-traffic control. In a matter of months, military radars were pressed into service; within two years, Congress had created the Federal Aviation Agency (FAA)—later renamed the Federal Aviation Administration—to promote air safety. It was evident that computers were needed to process the huge volume of rapidly changing information about airliner positions, altitudes and speeds. So began the development of a huge computerized system that would come to span the United States and be linked to much of the rest of the world.

Clerical tasks were the first to be automated. Data from flight plans and position reports was manually entered into computers; the system then automatically printed flight-progress strips and sent the relevant information to the controllers through whose sectors the aircraft would pass. Next came the automation of the data entry itself; as improved radar was integrated into the system, the computers used the radar information to generate visual displays. For the first time, controllers had up-to-the-moment graphic representations of the relative positions of all the aircraft in their sectors. A computer system monitored weather reports, allowing controllers to advise pilots of changing conditions. Programmers also devised a so-called fail-safe system that employed a backup unit to respond to breakdowns of any sort—in the hardware, software or human controllers.

By the end of the 1980s, the programming for the ATC system had consumed approximately 800 person-years of work, resulting in more than 1.1 million lines of code; taken collectively, the software constitutes one of the largest computer programs in the world. Constantly in development, it will probably never be supplanted by a wholly new product; because the system must function reliably every minute of every day, changes can be introduced only piecemeal. And even as the ATC system moves toward total automation, there will always be a place for humans. The reason is reliability: Humans make mistakes, but machines fail. And when there are failures, the final line of defense is human control. In the words of one programmer who worked for 15 years on the ATC system, "The best computer in the world for correlating information and coming up with a decision is the human brain."

Programs
That Perform
Everyday Miracles

Complex software handles many highly critical facets of modern life, from protecting the lives of airplane passengers to overseeing billions of dollars in international currency transfers. And for millions of citizens in the industrialized world, the computer age is also evident in more mundane ways.

Software plays myriad small roles in the drama of daily life. Climate-control software regulates the heating and lighting systems in computerized office buildings. Graphics software sends colorful meteorological pictures flitting across computerized weather maps on the evening news. Programs that assemble recorded speech read directory assistance listings over the telephone, and mailing list software churns out millions of personalized letters for everything from lottery sweepstakes to real-estate offerings. Software manages the transaction when a driver fills up at an automated gas pump, when a department store clerk validates a shopper's credit card, when an out-of-town music lover or sports fan purchases tickets to a concert or a game. It is through everyday operations like these that software has woven itself into the fabric of modern life.

Frequently, such encounters with software involve large central computer systems serving many remote users at the same time. The individual often does not see anything that resembles a computer, and in many cases the computer receives its data through a mechanism that bears no resemblance to a keyboard or mouse. At a supermarket check-out, for example, the input device is an optical scanner built into the counter, and the computer's output includes a printed receipt vastly more detailed than those cranked out by old-fashioned mechanical cash registers. At a traffic-clogged downtown intersection, the input device is a magnetic coil, buried in the pavement, that counts cars passing over it; the output is an ever-changing array of WALK-DON'T WALK signs, green arrows, red lights and other visual cues.

The software encounters illustrated in the following pages all involve relatively small moments in everyday life — opening the mail, passing groceries through a supermarket checkout, placing a telephone call, waiting for a traffic light to change. But behind each of these moments lie thousands of lines of program code, carefully crafted to manage the detailed data flow that makes the event proceed smoothly.

Personal Letters from a Computer

Increasingly sophisticated techniques employed by direct mail advertisers have radically altered the letters — once addressed to an anonymous "Occupant" — that often jam mailboxes. Political fund-raisers, charitable organizations, magazine and catalogue publishers, insurance companies, clothing manufacturers and many other businesses that solicit orders through the mail have come to rely on computers to keep track of the millions of names on their mailing lists, to target specific customers and to give each of their advertisements and solicitations the look of a personal appeal.

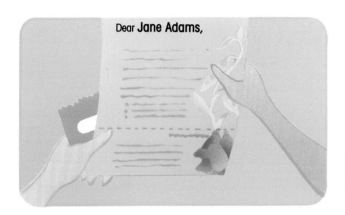

Dear **Jane Adams,**

A hypothetical customer, Jane Adams, receives a direct mail letter offering her membership in a gardening society. The text of the letter mentions her name and address, and refers to her family's fondness for gardening.

HOUSE LIST

Jane Adams
10 Taylor St.

Eric Andrews
25 Main St.

Philip Astor
2100 Madison Ave.

Sally Baxter
107 N. 33rd Ave.

RENTAL LIST

Jane Adams
10 Taylor St.

Leslie Adelman
502 Second St.

Gregory Alexander
1400 N. Lexington Rd.

T. S. Berman
609 Flower Ave.

MERGED LIST

Dear "NAME", The "LAST NAME" family of "STREET ADDRESS" has been chosen because of your interest in "STATE" horticulture to receive our culinary herb chart when you join our Society of Gardeners. In addition to this chart, suitable for framing, your membership includes these privileges:

More than likely, Jane Adams' name is on this mailing list because it has previously appeared on other lists. Direct mail advertisers compile their lists from two main sources — in-house lists based on data gathered directly by the company, and rental lists of people who have done business with other firms. Companies often run a package of in-house and rental lists through a merge/purge program designed to combine various lists into one, eliminating duplicate names. The program can also select appropriate zip codes to ensure that urban apartment dwellers, for example, do not receive mailings for products aimed at ranchers and farmers. The program can also eliminate the names of individuals who wish to be removed from direct mail lists.

The advertiser writes a form letter, using special codes to order the mailing list program to insert each customer's name, address and any other appropriate information. The software adjusts the text around the inserted words to make each form letter appear to have been printed individually.

The lists maintained by many direct mail advertisers are enormous data bases packed with information about each customer — age, credit history, income, previous mail order purchases and other details that help marketers fine-tune their advertising strategies. Direct mail companies use computers to sort and merge lists from several sources to produce new lists that match the specific characteristics they are looking for in their customers. Powerful word-processing software can now create individualized mailings that incorporate into the text not only a customer's name and address but other personal information as well. As illustrated here, a direct mail letter is composed by the computer from two sources of information. In one portion of its memory, the machine holds an electronic version of the basic letter; a piece of the customer list is stored in another memory location. The direct mail software plugs data for each customer into the appropriate spots in the letter, moving the rest of the text to leave exactly enough room for each insertion. Thus personalized, the letter is sent off to be printed.

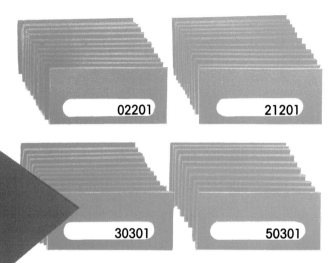

Dear **Gregory Alexander,**
The Alexander family of 1400 N. Lexington Road has been chosen be-cause of your interest in California

Dear **Jane Adams,**
The Adams family of 10 Taylor Street has been chosen because of your interest in Pennsylvania horticulture to receive our culinary herb chart when you join our Society of Gardeners. In addition to this chart, suitable for framing, your membership includes these privileges:

- A quarterly magazine
- A monthly newsletter
- Discounts on seeds and bulbs

Please fill out the coupon and send today!

ADA22205CHART678

SOCIETY OF GARDENERS COUPON

02201   21201

30301   50301

Direct mail software often incorporates a zip code sorting function that can save advertisers both postage and printing costs. Sorting letters qualifies an advertiser for bulk mail discount rates. A list can also be sorted to help advertisers zero in on residential areas that match target demographic characteristics.

When Jane Adams fills out her coupon and joins the gardening society, her response to this mailing will be recorded in the society's customer file, where it will now become data for software to evaluate in the compilation of future lists.

Printed on the customer's mail-back coupon is a serial number called the key line. Coded for such data as zip code and the type of material included in the mailing, the key line helps the advertiser analyze responses to its mailing. This analysis adds valuable information to a firm's customer files, enabling the firm to refine its own advertising, and making its in-house mailing list an attractive rental for other companies.

OUTGOING MAIL

Codes for a More Efficient Marketplace

The alternating thick and thin bars of a Universal Product Code (UPC) symbol are an identification number transformed by the check-out stand scanner (*below*) into electrical impulses and then translated into ones and zeros for the computer. The number on the label is written out twice, once in common decimal digits, once in bar code notation. Usually, the first half of a UPC number identifies the manufacturer, the second half identifies the product.

The computer checks the UPC number in a price file in the program's data base and sends two commands to the cash register. The name, price and other information on the item are flashed on the display screen and printed on the register tape. The computer may also flash special messages, reminding the clerk, for example, to check the age of anyone buying beer or wine.

Thank you for shopping
SUPERMART

TUNA	.99	T
SWISS CHEESE	1.29	T
LARGE A EGGS	.89	T
DELI	2.99	T
WHEAT BREAD	1.09	T
1.16lb @ 2lb/.99		
BANANAS	.57	T
H V VINEGAR	1.49	T

H V Vinegar $1.49

0   4

12345 67890

laser scanner light

Every time a supermarket clerk passes an item over the beeping scanner at the check-out stand, a sophisticated system of software goes into action. The scanner reads data encoded on a special label and passes the information along to a computer in the store. In less time than a human operator would take to ring up a sale on a cash register, the computer prints the item and its price on the customer's receipt. Almost simultaneously, it revises figures for the store's inventory and shelf space, giving managers an up-to-the-minute source of information regarding products that should be reordered to keep pace with customer demand. The system can thus help managers evaluate the success of advertising campaigns and otherwise improve the store's efficiency and profitability.

The key to this supermarket software is the Universal Product Code (UPC). Also called a bar code *(box, opposite)*, it is a system of identification numbers written in a form the computer can read with a stationary scanner like the one built into a check-out counter, or with a hand-held scanning wand passed over the clusters of wide and narrow lines. The same data-base-management software that organizes a supermarket's inventory can also be employed to keep track of machine parts on a factory's assembly line, logs floating downriver from a lumber camp — or runners crossing the finish line in a marathon.

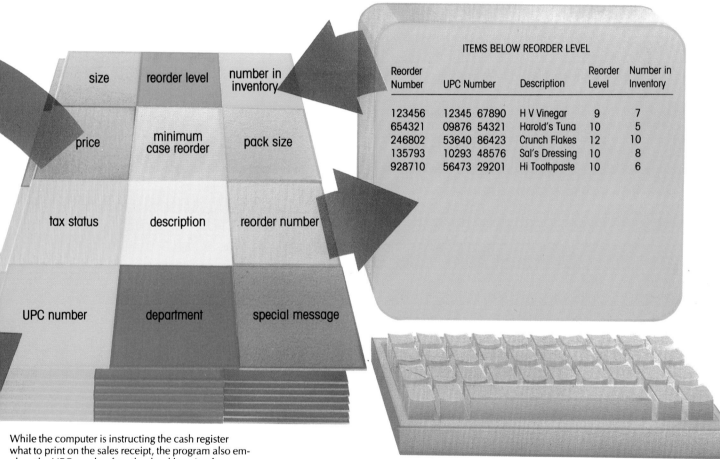

ITEMS BELOW REORDER LEVEL

Reorder Number	UPC Number	Description	Reorder Level	Number in Inventory
123456	12345 67890	H V Vinegar	9	7
654321	09876 54321	Harold's Tuna	10	5
246802	53640 86423	Crunch Flakes	12	10
135793	10293 48576	Sal's Dressing	10	8
928710	56473 29201	Hi Toothpaste	10	6

size / reorder level / number in inventory
price / minimum case reorder / pack size
tax status / description / reorder number
UPC number / department / special message

While the computer is instructing the cash register what to print on the sales receipt, the program also employs the UPC number for other bookkeeping functions. Every available piece of information about each product in the store is indexed in the data base. With each transaction, the computer takes note of a product's size, its sales tax status, whether there are any legal restrictions on its sale, whether the buyer used a coupon and a variety of other facts.

As each item is tallied at the check-out counter, the computer subtracts it from the store's inventory. By checking the minimum allowable inventory figure for that item, the computer determines whether it is time to reorder. The software is usually designed to hold inventory figures for the store manager to inspect at the end of the business day. Meanwhile, however, the manager can also keep the system up to date by entering other information such as price changes and new shipments.

An Operator's Electronic Aide

Over the years, directory assistance operators answering requests for telephone numbers have graduated from manually paging through phone books to using microfiche machines and more recently to computers. Computers are ideally suited to this task, which in essence means searching for a particular piece of data in a long list of similar items. And now computers can do more than just look a number up; thanks to powerful software, they can also read the number aloud.

Computer speech comes in two varieties, recorded and synthesized; both must be digitized, or turned into ones and zeros for the computer (box). Recorded voices are virtually indistinguishable from live human speech but require large amounts of memory: Eight thousand memory slots are needed to store one second of digitized recorded sound. Synthesized speech is made up of digitized phonemes, the 50 or so distinct sounds of spoken English; it requires less memory to store than recorded speech but can be less lifelike.

The number for
Edward Ryan,
please

The caller rings directory assistance, gives the operator the name of a city, then a name and address. The operator, seated at a special keyboard and display console, types in the data, then enters a command telling the system computer to search for the requested number.

The system computer, which serves as many as 600 operators simultaneously, uses database-management software to search through the millions of names and numbers in its memory. The software is set up to find similar-sounding names even when they are not similarly spelled. The operator types in the code for the correct listing and forwards it to an audio unit, which is controlled by another computer.

DIRECTORY	RHINE, RHYNE, RYON SECTION: RESIDENTIAL		3 SOUND ALIKES PRESENT OPERATOR CODE: 01526
Ryan. . . . Edward J	1455 Carmelle sq	482-1650	A
Ryan. . . . Edward L	8 Pine Villa rd	481-2990	B
Ryan. . . . Elizabeth	3706 Broadway	936-2261	C
Ryan. . . . Elmer F	1305 River rd	995-3273	D
Ryan. . . . Emma	2020 Queen	995-4695	E
Ryan. . . . Eugene	5915 Sandburg dr	997-2951	F
Ryan. . . . Eugenie	2908 Dabney st	997-6631	G

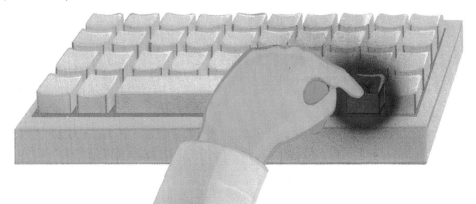

A Digitized Voice

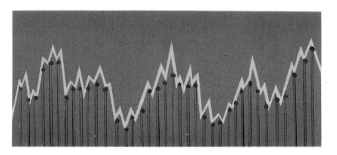

Treating the sounds of human speech so that the computer can deal with them is a matter of converting an analog signal — a continuous sound wave — into a sequence of discrete digital pieces, a process shown here in simplified form. To capture the nuances of the human voice, an analog-to-digital converter samples, or measures, the frequency, amplitude and other characteristics of the wave form at regular intervals thousands of times per second, assigning a precise numerical value to each sample. From this coded blueprint, the computer can reconstruct the sound electronically, translating the numerical values into electric voltages, which are then amplified to produce fragments of sound.

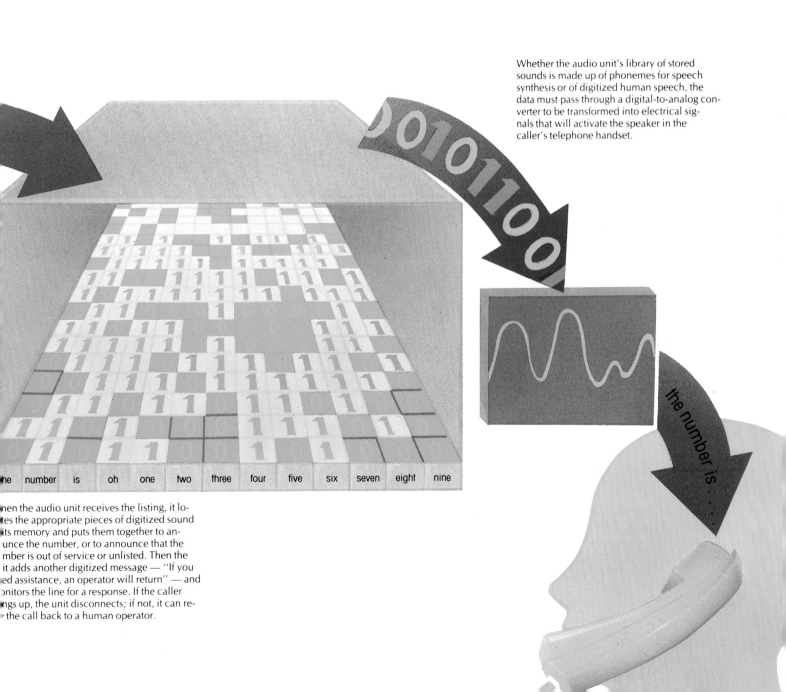

Whether the audio unit's library of stored sounds is made up of phonemes for speech synthesis or of digitized human speech, the data must pass through a digital-to-analog converter to be transformed into electrical signals that will activate the speaker in the caller's telephone handset.

the number is oh one two three four five six seven eight nine

the number is . . . . .

nen the audio unit receives the listing, it lo-
tes the appropriate pieces of digitized sound
its memory and puts them together to an-
unce the number, or to announce that the
mber is out of service or unlisted. Then the
it adds another digitized message — "If you
ed assistance, an operator will return" — and
onitors the line for a response. If the caller
ngs up, the unit disconnects; if not, it can re-
the call back to a human operator.

A Traffic Maestro

In the decades since the mid-1950s, when the invention of an automated system of traffic controls dramatically reduced congestion in the streets of Denver, Colorado, traffic engineers have seized on advances in computer science to construct flexible, multipurpose systems capable of responding rapidly to a wide variety of traffic situations. These systems can automatically adjust for rush hour at a predetermined time every morning and evening, and can sort out the automotive chaos that often snarls up the streets around a large stadium or cultural center. Colorful graphics enable traffic engineers at a central computer to supervise traffic flow at a critical intersection, pinpoint dangerous trouble spots and handle emergency situations by remote control.

Motorists at computerized intersections provide input to a traffic-control program as their cars pass over sensors buried in the roadway. These sensors, the nerve endings of the system, note the number of cars on the road. Given this data, augmented by readings from its own internal clock, the computer can calculate where the traffic is heavy and how fast it is moving. As traffic volume and flow patterns change, the computer is programmed to alter the timing sequences of the traffic and pedestrian signals.

Traffic-control software can eliminate some of the irritations that accompany driving in crowded metropolitan areas and save lives as well. Keeping traffic flowing smoothly can reduce the number of fender-benders and more serious rear-end collisions, whether on downtown streets or on high-speed freeways. And in some cities, special preemptive systems ensure that ambulances, fire engines and other emergency vehicles will have clear streets when lost time could prove fatal.

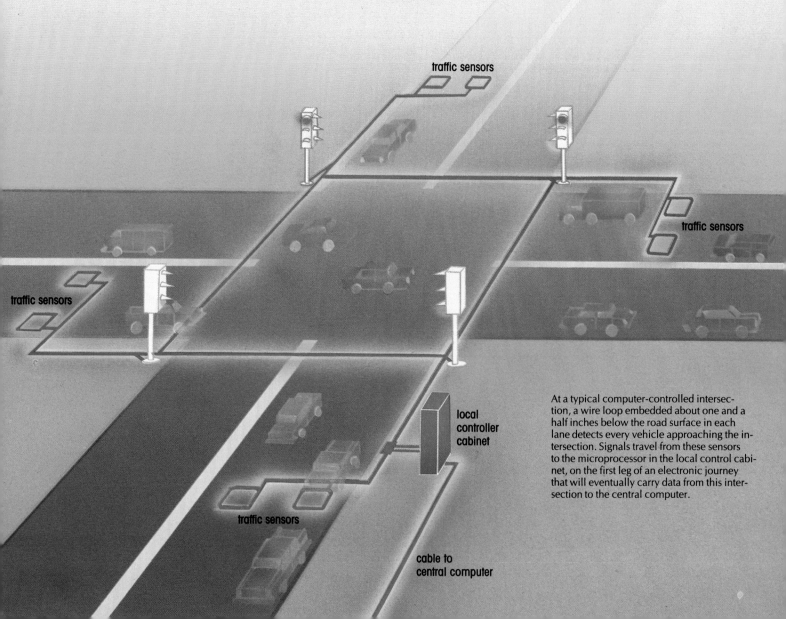

traffic sensors

traffic sensors

traffic sensors

traffic sensors

local controller cabinet

At a typical computer-controlled intersection, a wire loop embedded about one and a half inches below the road surface in each lane detects every vehicle approaching the intersection. Signals travel from these sensors to the microprocessor in the local control cabinet, on the first leg of an electronic journey that will eventually carry data from this intersection to the central computer.

cable to central computer

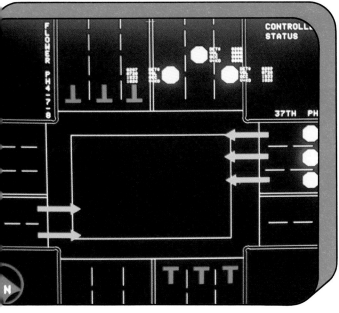

In a "time-of-day" traffic program, the timing of traffic lights is adjusted throughout the day and week to deal with regular fluctuations such as rush hours. Color-coded symbols on a monitor screen allow traffic engineers at a central location to note traffic volume *(yellow circles)*, signal changes *(green arrows and red stop symbols)* and other traffic flow data.

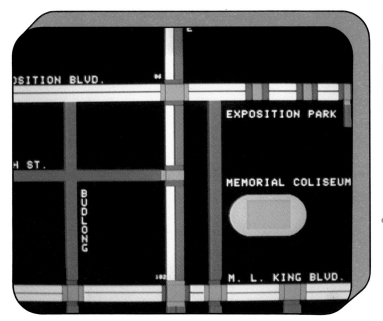

"Traffic-responsive" programs work according to the amount of traffic. Programmed with several different timing patterns for traffic signals, the computer chooses one based on actual conditions. Unlike time-of-day plans, which deal with predictable fluctuations in volume, traffic-responsive plans are meant for areas with irregular fluctuations, such as the streets around a shopping mall or a sports arena. Imposed on the intersections above, a traffic-responsive plan would help reduce congestion *(red lane)* near the coliseum.

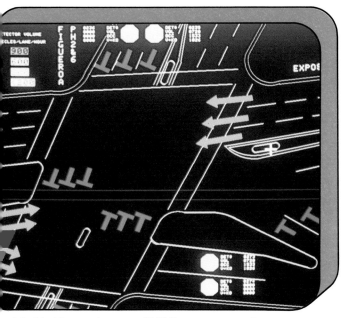

A "critical-intersection-control" (CIC) program customizes the timing of the lights at special locations, such as this intersection of several major arteries. Rather than selecting a preset timing plan from an array of available options, as a traffic-responsive program does, CIC software monitors traffic volume second by second and times each intersection in conjunction with relevant nearby intersections.

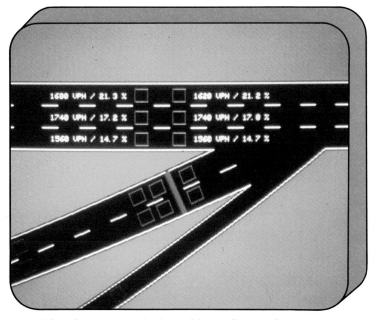

Where freeway congestion is a problem, traffic-control software can adjust entrance ramp lights to keep traffic moving smoothly. A ramp-metering program analyzes signals from sensors embedded in both the ramp and the freeway, and regulates the cycle of red and green ramp lights to allow cars onto the freeway at optimal intervals.

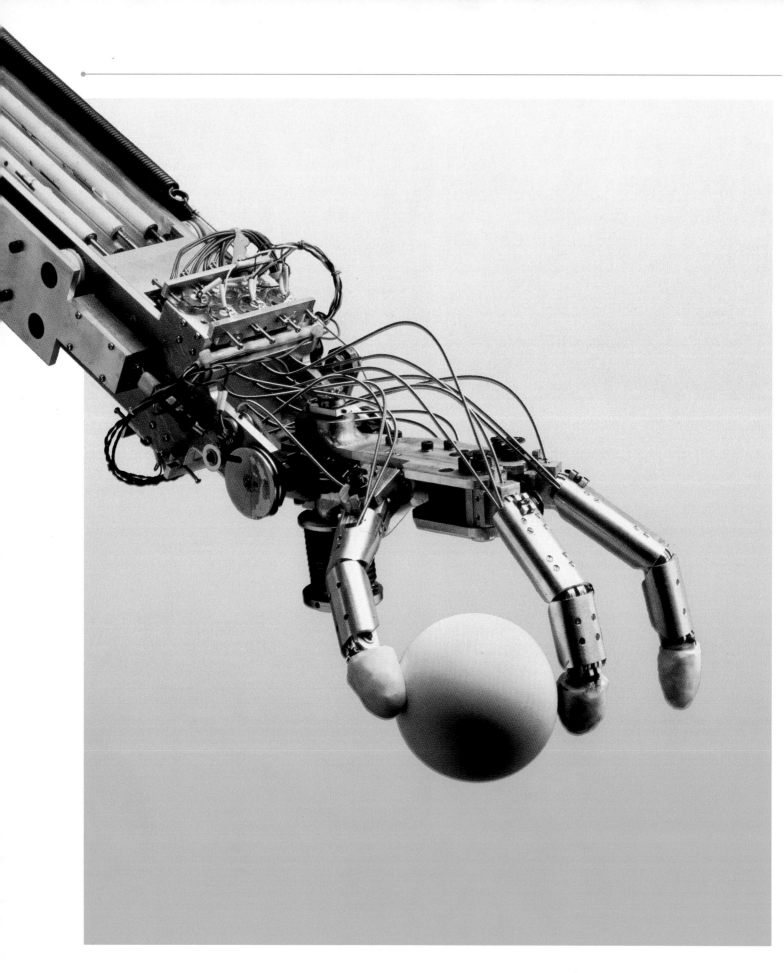

Ever-moving Frontiers

HAL, the omniscient computer in the science fiction epic *2001: A Space Odyssey*, could speak, hear and seemingly think exactly like his human colleagues aboard their Jupiter-bound spaceship. In addition to serving as the ship's full-time automatic pilot, he played a superior game of chess and was a facile conversationalist who could even read lips., He also exhibited such regrettable human traits as conceit and paranoia. When HAL turned malevolent and began killing off members of the crew, the survivors countered by performing a kind of digital lobotomy on him—cutting off his higher functions and limiting his role to monitoring the spacecraft's mechanical systems.

Despite his antisocial tendencies, HAL seized the imagination of moviegoers when *2001* appeared in 1968. The notion of smart machines helping to run the world was exciting, even if it raised concerns about who—or what—might really be in control of such a world. These were not fanciful matters. A number of computer scientists predicted that the development of truly intelligent computers was just a matter of time, and two decades later, many remain confident that something like HAL may indeed be with us by the early 21st Century. Although formidable problems remain—especially in perfecting vision and hearing, areas in which HAL was so proficient—computers have already achieved a level of sophistication and power scarcely thought possible in the era of UNIVAC I and other first-generation machines.

Many of the jobs routinely performed by today's computers recall the musings of yesterday's science fiction. Space exploration, the study of distant galaxies and global communications as we know them would be impossible without computers. Powerful supercomputers—with their associated software—are coming to grips with the awesome complexities involved in weather forecasting. Using the versatile tool of computer simulation, scientists grapple with the management of ocean fisheries and other of the world's resources. On a smaller scale, computer software has entered the fields of medicine and psychology, helping doctors to diagnose diseases and therapists to probe their patients' psyches. In more esoteric applications, researchers are turning to computers for fundamental clues about the evolution of the universe and the origins of life. And in a kind of "bootstrap" process, computer scientists are relying on the current generation of machines for essential help in designing and building the next generation of computers.

The men and women toiling on the frontiers of computer science face many problems that may seem at first glance to be little more than the rarefied cogitations of ivory-tower academics. And yet these puzzles, which may be theoretical in nature and which are often cast in colorful metaphors, can have quite concrete applications in the real worlds of technology and business.

In a masterly display of a programmer's skill, robot fingers grip a fragile egg with nearly human gentleness. The 14 joints in the wrist and fingers of this experimental hand-and-arm assembly are flexed by microcomputer-controlled actuators in the device's forearm; complex software determines how much pressure the joints should exert.

101

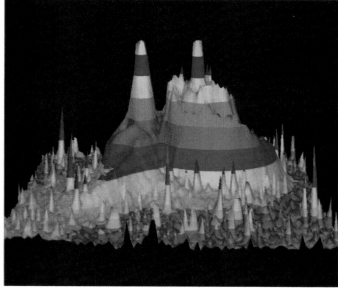

Twenty million light-years away from earth, the Whirlpool galaxy and a smaller galactic companion show up as roiled swirls of brilliance in a conventional optical photograph *(above, left)*. But a computer-generated image *(above)* reveals intricate variations of luminosity within each galaxy. The central peaks represent regions of greatest brightness; the spikes ringing the galactic nuclei are individual stars.

The "traveling salesman problem," for example, vexed traditional mathematicians for years before it was taken up more recently by computer scientists. In this hypothetical situation, a traveling salesman is about to start off on a cross-country selling trip. The trick is to arrange his itinerary so that he travels the least number of miles while on his way from city to city. The problem is easy enough to solve if the number of cities involved is small—say, no more than a dozen. But if the number is large, arriving at an answer is virtually impossible; even a powerful computer could take years—maybe centuries—to decide on an optimum route if the number of cities is in the hundreds. This is because the number of potential routes grows exponentially, with the exponent in the equation being the number of cities to be visited. Under these circumstances, the number of routes to be tested can easily grow into the billions.

The traveling salesman problem and similar conundrums belong to the expanding branch of computer science known as complexity theory. Researchers in this field seek to write the simplest possible algorithms for solving problems that deal with the efficient routing of something through a network—be it an electrical signal or a freight train. Cracking these problems, therefore, can yield big benefits to telephone companies, freight haulers and computer firms concerned with the wiring of microchips that may contain hundreds of thousands of circuits on a quarter-inch sliver of silicon.

MODELING WEATHER

Perhaps no mental task is better suited to the computer's power—or more in need of complex software—than weather forecasting. In the late 1940s, computer pioneer John von Neumann recognized that equations representing the fluid dynamics of atmospheric movement could be assembled into a larger mathematical model of a weather system and solved on a computer. (While meteorologists had employed simple mathematical models in their work before, the amount of data they could use was severely limited, since all the equations had to be worked out by hand.) At the Institute for Advanced Study, von Neumann built a machine that cut the time it took to produce 24-hour forecasts from 24 hours to just a few minutes.

Although von Neumann demonstrated the first practical application of a computer in making weather predictions, the idea had actually been suggested decades earlier by a prescient English meteorologist named Lewis Richardson. In 1922 Richardson tried to imagine a futuristic forecasting center. In his wishful vision he saw a huge room filled with 64,000 human "computers" busily solving equations with slide rules and mechanical calculators. Each person was responsible for equations representing one part of the globe. To ensure that the equations were solved in the proper sequence, a master meteorologist stood on a tall pillar and controlled the flow. This director, wrote Richardson, "is like the conductor of an orchestra, in which the instruments are slide-rules and calculating machines. But instead of waving a baton, he turns a beam of rosy light upon any region that is running ahead, and a beam of blue upon those who are behind."

Today's complex world makes accurate forecasting even more of a necessity than it was in Richardson's day. During a typical year in the United States, for example, the vagaries of weather — hurricanes, floods, freezes, hail and lightning — cost property owners and farmers many billions of dollars, and accounted for thousands of injuries and hundreds of deaths. Small wonder that many farmers and businesses subscribe to private weather services, or that a half billion calls are placed each year to telephone weather numbers.

GATHERING THE DATA

Richardson's dream of computer-based forecasting coincided with the beginnings of modern meteorology. The technology of the 1920s was sufficiently advanced to allow for the accurate, systematic collecting of weather data. Meteorologists — at first intermittently, but eventually on a daily basis — began sending aloft helium balloons equipped with devices for recording temperature, humidity and pressure at various levels in the region of the lower atmosphere known as the troposphere. Today, a worldwide network collects data from thousands of points and feeds the information to major weather centers for analysis. At weather stations throughout North America, scientists probe the skies with balloon-borne instruments and at least eight times a day take ground readings of temperature, humidity, barometric pressure and rainfall. Satellites, airliners and ships at sea contribute to the data flood. In all, the U.S. National Meteorological Center located in Camp Springs, Maryland, receives hundreds of thousands of measurements every day.

Processing this torrent of information requires some of the most powerful computers in the world. These so-called supercomputers may cost tens of millions of dollars and can crunch data at the extraordinary rate of as many as a billion computations per second. Tremendous speed and power are essential, because the mathematical models used in weather forecasting—the supercomputer's software—are among the most complex programs ever devised. Far beyond the capacities of even the most inspired individuals, such software is written by teams of programmers, each working on a single part, or module, of the larger model, and frequently residing in different cities.

A global weather model works by dividing the troposphere into discrete units, or cells. Usually, these are 100 to 200 miles on a side, although the most advanced of the world's weather centers, the European Centre for Medium Range Forecasts in Reading, England, employs a model whose cells are 75 miles on a side. (The Cray X-MP supercomputer at Reading engorges data four times a day, chews it for 50 minutes and then spits out projections that extend 10 days ahead.) The cells are also divided vertically: The European model is broken down into 19 levels from ground to mid-ozone layer, about 20 miles above the earth. The computer model for each cell contains equations representing weather components such as wind, cloud cover, and the presence or absence of mountains. The equations within a cell are interrelated, and all the cells in the model are linked so that, as if in a meteorological spreadsheet, a change in one can influence what happens in another.

In the real world, for example, an increase in wind speed over the ocean off San Francisco might raise humidity, triggering rain that could cause a temperature change affecting the heat balance in the atmosphere. This in turn might affect the direction of westerly wind currents. A cell's computer equations would represent every step in this chain of events, and the model would project how new conditions in this cell might alter conditions two days later in the cell over Kansas City, 1,800 miles to the east.

While it may come as a surprise to anyone who hears a report for sunny skies and two hours later gets drenched by a thunderstorm, weather forecasting has in fact improved dramatically in recent years—largely as a result of computers. On a global scale, forecasts for periods of up to five and six days ahead have become as accurate as two-day forecasts were in the 1970s. And in predicting temperatures over a 24-hour period, the number of errors exceeding 10° F. is now half what it was in the 1960s.

The less frequent but still galling inaccuracies that continue to plague forecasters have several causes that far transcend the capabilities of computer software. The first is simply a lack of sufficient data. While the global weather network is extremely sophisticated, the data sources are still too few and far between. Large gaps in the network occur over expanses of tropical ocean, where some of the worst weather originates. Meteorologists also lament the coarseness of their weather models, whose individual cells cover too large an area to achieve pinpoint precision at the local level. "Even though we can predict the possibility of thunderstorms over Kansas with some accuracy," notes William Bonner, director of the U.S. National Meteorological Center, "will one develop over Kansas City? And when?" Robert Bunting, a scientist at the government's Environmental Re-

search Laboratories in Boulder, Colorado, observes that the current network "is like a whale net, while many of the storms that really matter are minnows."

The other cause of inaccuracies — and a problem that appears, for the time being at least, less solvable — is the difficulty of modeling fluid flows. The complication lies in what mathematicians call the "chaotic" nature of fluid dynamics. The equations required to describe atmospheric changes, for example, are known as nonlinear partial differential equations; while a linear equation such as $y = x + 5$ always produces a straight line when plotted on a graph, an equation such as $y = x + x(dy/dx) + x(d^2y/dx^2)$ might plot a far less orderly series of points. Furthermore, even a minor error in the value of one of the variables can send the equation careering toward an entirely different solution than it might otherwise have.

THE AMPLIFICATION OF AN ERROR

Meteorologists have recognized this problem since at least 1960, when Edward Lorenz of MIT programmed a computer to solve a simple model of the earth's atmosphere. Lorenz ran the model several times and was staggered to find that as small a change as rounding off some figures from six decimal places to three produced completely different results. "I knew right then that if the real atmosphere behaved like this, long-range weather forecasting was impossible," he said. That gloomy conclusion means that even the smallest error in a piece of data — a temperature reading that is off by a degree, for instance — can grow during the course of the calculation to monstrous proportions, spelling the difference between a forecast for sunny skies two weeks hence or for torrential rains. "The consequence of measuring with only finite precision," says physicist James Crutchfield of the University of California at Berkeley "is that the measurements are just not good enough: chaos takes them and blows them up in your face." Today, the study of chaotic systems as diverse as weather and the boom-and-bust cycle of insect pests has developed into a minor growth industry among research scientists, who hope to find some underlying order in the seeming randomness of such events. For now, however, the best they can do in dealing with chaos is to treat it statistically — to predict the probability that some event (such as a snowstorm) will occur on a given day. Until some breakthrough is achieved, meteorologists have placed the outer limit for reasonably accurate forecasting at two weeks.

Improving medium-range forecasts (those between three days and two weeks) will depend on finer-grained models and more data — from additional weather stations and new and more sophisticated instruments, including weather satellites and advanced types of weather radar. Much faster and more powerful computers in turn will be needed to handle the expansion of data, since a tenfold increase in a model's resolution requires a ten-thousandfold jump in computer speed. Computers fast enough to achieve such an increase probably will not be available until the final decade of the century.

Improving long-range forecasts — those beyond the theoretical limit of two weeks — will take all of the above and then some. The U.S. National Weather Service already makes 30- and 90-day forecasts, but these are statistical predictions that do little more than prophesy variations from average temperature and rainfall. And even for such general parameters as these, the National Weather

omputer enhancement of this infrared satellite view of the earth assigns colors to certain temperature ranges; here, green indicates low temperatures. Such large-scale images aid meteorologists in tracking global weather patterns and making short-range predictions.

Service is correct only about 65 per cent of the time. Significantly, these long-range projections are based not on computer models but on traditional meteorological analysis. The problem again is the chaotic nature of weather systems.

Yet, meteorologists remain hopeful that they will eventually be able to make accurate, computer-based forecasts beyond two weeks. To test the feasibility of this goal, two Cyber 205 supercomputers at Princeton's Geophysical Fluid Dynamics Laboratory have been harnessed to a global weather model that combines data from the ocean with atmospheric measurements. The lab's work, sponsored by the National Oceanographic and Atmospheric Administration, is devoted largely to developing programming techniques for long-range forecasts.

The goal of the Princeton scientists is to produce reliable seasonal forecasts of temperature and rainfall. The lab has access to several years' worth of weather data gathered from all over the world, which it plugs into the tens of thousands of equations in its weather model. Programmers constantly tinker with the model in attempts to refine it—for example, by changing the mathematical "shapes" of mountaintops from smooth to jagged, which better simulates their effect on overhead winds.

The laboratory has made progress in fathoming the inscrutable and seemingly random forces governing long-range weather patterns. Along with other meteorologists struggling with the problem, the researchers at Princeton are encouraged by certain recurring phenomena such as "blocking," the unpredictable slowing of wind currents in the upper troposphere. By disrupting normal patterns, blocking can produce devastating droughts and prolonged hot and cold spells. Scientists still do not understand blocking well enough to be able to program its occurrence—a significant weakness in the computer models. At the same time, the persistence of blocking offers hope that the atmosphere may be governed by some deeper rhythm that may ultimately prove predictable.

"It's the things the models do wrong in a repeatful way that are encouraging to me," observes Reading meteorologist Adrian Simmons. "If it was just the usual cyclones and anticyclones forming and reforming, it wouldn't be so hopeful. But because some of these systems *are* long-lived, one feels sort of intuitively that they should be predictable."

Balancing that view is a cautionary one from Kiku Miyakoda, leader of the Princeton group. No matter how sophisticated our computer models become, he says, "I believe that weather was invented by God and that there are certain features of it that we'll never understand."

ACTION-PACKED GRAPHICS

If weather models are a little-known and esoteric branch of computer software, video games remain among the most visible and popular uses of software. At their most elaborate, these games transport their human players into fantasy worlds to do digital battle with alien invaders or prehistoric monsters, all brought to life through the magic of computer graphics.

This technology has its serious and practical applications as well. One popular program designed for home computers, Flight Simulator, was originally created as a video game, but proved so realistic that many people wound up using it to decide whether to take actual flying lessons. The program's graphics show the control panel of a Cessna 182 and, through a simulated cockpit windshield, an

Sitting at the controls of a computer-operated helicopter flight simulator, a trainee sees this vivid panorama of high-tension wires, trees and another helicopter through the cockpit windshield. The simulator's detailed program can project the equivalent of 10,000 miles of realistic terrain, re-creating almost any situation a pilot might face in actual flight.

airport panorama. The dials of the control panel and the view of the approaching runway change according to the signals transmitted by a joystick manipulated by the armchair pilot. With Flight Simulator and similar programs, the pilot can vary the weather and the time of day to practice flying under different conditions.

Much larger and more elaborate simulators are used by commercial airlines, the military and NASA for training pilots and astronauts in the high-tech skills needed for flying jet aircraft and the space shuttle. At the Johnson Space Center in Houston, NASA's $40 million Shuttle Mission Simulator (SMS) is a self-contained world in which computer software mimics every phase—and potential problem—of a shuttle flight. A windowless capsule, the SMS sits 15 feet off the ground, atop a moving hydraulic platform that makes the capsule pitch, roll and turn like the real space shuttle in flight. Its mechanics are similar to those of other simulators that have been used for years in training pilots for conventional craft. What is so dazzlingly different about the SMS is the realism achieved by its advanced technology.

An astronaut crew works on a mock-up flight deck that exactly replicates the real thing on the space shuttle. The program controlling the SMS's "flight" does a second-by-second countdown to lift-off and reproduces digital readouts and graphic displays for every phase of a flight. From the simulator's cockpit, everything looks just as it would on launch from Cape Canaveral, in earth orbit or during a landing on the desert runway at Edwards Air Force Base in California. The pilot sees the flash of rocket ignition on lift-off and the launch pad falling away; minutes later, another flash signals the separation of rocket boosters. The blue sky darkens and stars come out as the shuttle lifts beyond the atmosphere.

Not unexpectedly, much of the SMS's time is taken up in preparing astronauts to deal with mechanical failures, ranging from minor malfunctions to major emergencies that could abort a mission. The system can be programmed to simulate almost any contingency, including loss of the shuttle's onboard computers or the blast of a 150-mile-per-hour crosswind as the 102-ton craft glides in for a landing. The SMS is so important to the space shuttle program that it is generally in use around the clock, seven days a week. A typical four-hour training session is sufficiently realistic that even veteran astronauts emerge from the simulator sweating and exhausted.

The actual space shuttle, of course, is absolutely dependent on computers for monitoring its vital functions and precisely guiding its flight. The craft has a total of five onboard computers, four of which are constantly kibitzing one another. Should any one of the four start producing results that vary from those of the other three, it would automatically shut down. If this happened again so that only two computers remained functioning, the fifth—made by a different manufacturer and programmed by a different team of computer scientists—would go into action. Its software is designed to take over full control of the mission.

VIDEO WARFARE

If computer simulation has proved an invaluable tool in the space program, it has also been useful in military training—most notably in a software tour de force called Janus. Named for the two-faced god who guarded the gates of Rome, Janus puts opposing generals on a video battlefield in which all the components of modern land war—including artillery, tanks, aircraft and tactical nuclear weapons—can be brought into play. Located at Lawrence Livermore National Laboratory in California and at the U.S. Army War College in Carlisle, Pennsylvania, the $2.45-million project can pull from its huge data base a topographical map of any 15-mile-square plot on earth. Usually, though, the game is played on turf along the border between East and West Germany, where NATO strategists believe any U.S.-Soviet confrontation would be most likely to occur.

War games have been played since at least 3000 B.C., when Chinese warlords moved stones around a stylized map in a game known as *Wei-Hai*. For most of the succeeding five millennia, generals fought their board battles in much the same way, by maneuvering wooden blocks representing friendly and enemy forces. But the computer age changed all that forever. With their ability to store huge amounts of information and to display and manipulate it on a video screen, computers offer today's commanders a fantastic tool for mimicking the complex details of modern war.

A typical Janus scenario might project on the computer monitor a patch of terrain complete with rivers, mountains, roads and towns. Each of the opposing commanders—American and Soviet—has his own screen, which displays only the information about the enemy that he would be likely to have during a real battle. As the players move their forces by maneuvering mouselike pucks on electronic graphics boards, the action unfolds simultaneously on the screen. The computer executes two million instructions per second, calculating the flight times of artillery shells to the millisecond and even figuring the reloading times for specific weapons. Should the players resort to nuclear weapons, the machine would take weather conditions such as wind and humidity into account when it calculated the spread of a fireball.

One American officer might be in charge of a bridge guarding a strategic valley threatened from the east by Soviet tanks. When intelligence reports warn that the Soviets are moving toward the valley, the officer dispatches a squadron of A-10 ground-attack planes—represented on the screen by blue symbols—to investigate. As the aircraft approach a pass leading into the valley, the pilots spot the Soviet forces, indicated by red symbols that show up on the screen only when the Soviet tanks come into the line of sight of the American pilots. (The computer calculates this from data representing topographical details and the planes' altitude.) Meanwhile, the American planes draw fire from the Soviets; when one of the A-10s is knocked out, it is instantly replaced on the screen by the symbol C for casualty. Under withering Soviet antiaircraft fire, three of the downed pilot's companions meet the same fate. Because the planes are the eyes of the U.S. commander, most of the Soviet forces are rendered invisible—and disappear from the screen.

With four of the six American aircraft down, the Soviet tanks push on and begin pounding the U.S. forward positions. White dots appear on the screen wherever a shell or missile lands, and when one of the missiles explodes close to an American platoon, the unit is replaced by another ominous C. Another close shot, however, miraculously leaves the Americans unscathed; true to the vagaries of war, the Janus programmers allow each commander a certain measure of luck.

But it is surprise and superior firepower—not fortune—that eventually rule the day. The American forces are soon decimated, and the Soviets take control of the valley. It is an object lesson in the importance of air support that the losing officer will not soon forget.

A FUTURE ON THE FRONT LINE

Although Janus was designed as a training device, military planners also see it as a tool that might one day be adapted for frontline duty as a kind of superbrain for pressured commanders coping with the pace and complexity of battle. Already computers appear destined to play an ever-larger role in the future of combat systems. An advanced jet fighter like the U.S. Air Force's F-16 literally cannot get off the ground without the assistance of its four onboard computers, and once airborne, it depends on the same computers to fly straight. Tens of thousands of computers would be required to operate the proposed Strategic Defense Initiative, an orbiting antimissile system.

The Pentagon hopes that Janus and similar programs are bellwethers for even more sophisticated military computer systems of the future. In addition to having much larger memories, a generation of computer systems now under development would be able—like humans—to make informed guesses based on incomplete or even inaccurate intelligence. Achieving this level of intuitive thinking in a machine is no mean task; it represents one of the frontiers of programming science. Physicist Edward Taylor of TRW of Redondo Beach, California, one of the companies working on the problem, explains it this way: "Take the game of chess, which in some ways resembles a military exercise. Various computer programs have been invented for playing chess, and some of them are pretty good. But suppose a chess-playing computer not only had to take into account the rules of the game, the positions of the players and the outcome of possible moves, but also had to deal with uncertainty. Imagine the computer confronting an opposing piece and not knowing for sure whether the piece were a rook or a pawn. That's a situation that faces soldiers all the time, and they deal with it by thinking about past experiences and making educated guesses — not necessarily optimum solutions. People can handle guesses, but most computer programs cannot."

Although they are sometimes stymied by ambiguities, computers are already able to evaluate information and draw conclusions concerning a given subject — as long as the facts are presented in a structured, logical way. Software capable of performing such tasks is known as an expert system. Expert systems are based mainly on deductive reasoning. That is, given a large body of facts, the expert system works through it by following prescribed rules.

Basic scientific research as well as fields as diverse as medicine and mineral exploration all use expert systems. Designers of such systems may interview scores of experts in a given area, culling from them the knowledge of their subject gained from a lifetime's work and then committing it to the software's data base. The computer thus confers a kind of immortality, preserving not only an individual's storehouse of facts but his or her rules of thumb for doing the job.

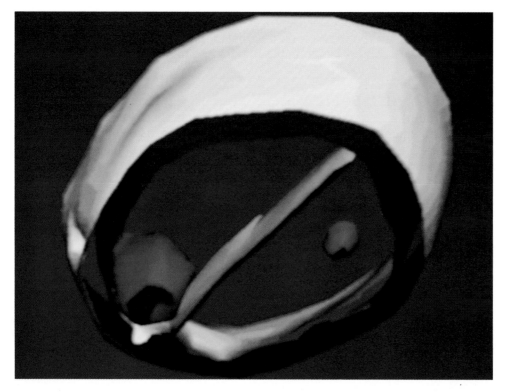

Two brain tumors are shown in red in a computer-generated cross section of a patient's head. The image was created from data collected by a CAT scanner, then color-enhanced by a computer to distinguish brain tissues of different densities. When making decisions about surgery or other courses of treatment, physicians can use sophisticated software to rotate such images and view them from any angle.

Many early expert systems were experiments with little practical impact. Internist-1, for example, was a medical-diagnosis program developed at the University of Pittsburgh in the 1970s. With this expert system, physicians could respond to increasingly detailed questions about a patient's symptoms and test results until the computer arrived at one or more possible diagnoses, ranked in order of probability. Doctors using the system could ask the computer how it reached its conclusion, and if the program erred they could enter new data to improve its performance. When completed in 1980, Internist-1 held information covering 5,000 variations of 650 diseases. Yet doctors, reluctant at that time to rely on a computer's analysis of symptoms, rarely used the system.

Like science itself, such experimental systems have an organic quality, continuing to evolve as they are modified and updated with new information. For example, a short-lived but quite effective mineral-exploration program known as Prospector was created at the Stanford Research Institute in 1976 from interviews with a handful of leading economic geologists. Its data base was updated and expanded annually until, by the end of the project in 1982, it contained the collective wisdom of several dozen authorities in this field. The program scored a dramatic and well-publicized success in its last year when it analyzed the geological features of an area in eastern Washington State and pinpointed the location of what turned out to be a major deposit of molybdenum, a mineral important in the manufacture of high-strength steel.

REASONING LIKE A SCIENTIST

More recently, computer scientists have been trying to equip expert systems with the power to reason inductively. This is the way scientists think when generalizing from experimental data to arrive at theories of universal laws, usually expressed as mathematical equations such as $F = ma$ or $E = mc^2$. One of the most promising of these programs is Bacon, developed in the late 1970s by Patrick Langley of Carnegie-Mellon University and named after the Elizabethan philosopher Francis Bacon, an early proponent of experimentation and the inductive method. Supplied with data from famous scientific experiments, the Bacon program was able, in effect, to rediscover such major principles as Kepler's third law of planetary motion, Boyle's law of gases, Snell's law of light refraction, Black's law of specific heat and Ohm's law in electricity. No expert system has discovered a new law, for science has become a lot more complex than it was in Ohm's or Kepler's day. But some computer scientists are confident that future versions of Bacon or similar programs will be able to do so.

Expert systems date from about 1965, when Stanford computer scientists Edward Feigenbaum and Bruce Buchanan joined forces with biochemist and Nobel laureate Joshua Lederberg to devise a computer-based system for determining the molecular structures of chemical compounds. In building the system, called DENDRAL, their first task was to create a program—founded on the simple but powerful system of Aristotelian logic—that posed a series of "if-then" questions representing basic rules about how atoms bond. With the framework established, they fleshed it out by adding facts about chemical compounds and the mental procedures human biochemists use to arrive at their decisions. This "knowledge engineering" was accomplished by interviewing biochemists about their thought processes while they worked through problems. Feigenbaum,

Buchanan and Lederberg refined the program by applying it to problems with known answers, checking the results and modifying the software accordingly.

Expanding on what they had learned, DENDRAL's creators soon produced a spin-off called Meta-DENDRAL—an expert system for assisting in building other expert systems. Among the many other systems that followed in DENDRAL's wake were MYCIN, for diagnosing serious bacterial infections and helping select antibiotics; PUFF, a diagnostic tool for lung diseases; ONCOCIN, for prescribing cancer therapy; and Molgen and Genesis, for assisting molecular biologists in planning DNA experiments and experiments in cloning.

Expert systems are the most successful application so far of the branch of computer science known as artificial intelligence. The term was coined during a two-month summer conference at Dartmouth in 1956, but the idea of "thinking machines" goes back at least to 700 B.C., when Egyptians turned for advice to talking icons (in reality, carved figures with priests hidden behind them). In the early days of research in artificial intelligence—or AI, as it is more familiarly known—proponents issued heady predictions about its possibilities, claiming that computers would soon be able to reason and to solve problems as well as any human. This has not happened, of course, and many AI researchers now believe it may be centuries before computers can think intuitively and cope with all of the nuances, ambiguities and logical contradictions that humans deal with routinely in everyday life. Even the most sophisticated expert system is little more than an idiot savant—a whiz in its area of expertise but hopeless outside it.

AI researchers continue to develop more sophisticated programs like Bacon, which can mimic at least certain aspects of inductive thought. They have also made progress in creating software that enables computers to respond to spoken commands or to recognize shapes and patterns. Programs for computer hearing and vision work by template matching, a process in which words or images are converted to digital models for comparison with other models stored in the computer's memory. The software has progressed to the point where it is used successfully, albeit in extremely restricted domains. Some factories, for example, employ machines to check the wiring of circuit boards. But there is not a computer in the world capable of determining that one human face in front view is in fact identical to the same face viewed from even a slightly different angle.

Indeed, one of the unexpected benefits of AI research has been to foster a renewed appreciation for the complexities of even the most elementary human thought processes. In the late 1960s and early 1970s, for example, researchers at MIT spent years programming a computer to follow simple keyboard commands instructing it to manipulate a pile of blocks generated on a computer screen. The computer was eventually able to stack and unstack the blocks about as well as a three-year-old child.

Spinning
a New View
of the Universe

One of the liveliest and most productive areas of computer science is graphics. High-tech graphics software has the power to generate images that furnish a wealth of insights into the physical world — and that often possess striking beauty and freshness, besides. Computer-generated models may represent anything from molecules to magnetic fields, suspension bridges to supersonic aircraft.

Such software is so complex that it typically requires hundreds of thousands of lines of instructions and years of development. Many programs, though displaying only a two-dimensional image on the video monitor, contain details of all three dimensions, thus enabling designers and researchers to view a particular model from many different perspectives. They also permit scientists to tinker with the shape of the model and to simulate the forces acting upon it.

The new techniques of modeling and simulation are revolutionizing industrial design. Structural engineers can perform stress tests on objects that are still a mere glimmering in their eye. Auto makers can simulate the effects of air resistance on a designer's conception for a car without ever constructing a physical prototype.

Even more exotic applications are finding a place in the laboratories of science. Researchers graphically simulate a cloud of gas whirling around a black hole or the circulation of water in the oceans' depths. Specialists in the new science of biomechanics help athletes run faster and jump higher and farther by analyzing nuances of technique. Plastic surgeons rehearse their operations on the computer, which lets them try out procedures and then see the results of their work before surgery begins. (In a similar application, researchers have even reconstructed the facial image of a 3,400-year-old Egyptian mummy.)

The most promising medical application of all may be disease prevention. Utilizing data derived from X-ray crystallography, expert programmers can create computer models delineating the structures of viruses. Such images may someday lead to protection against a host of human illnesses.

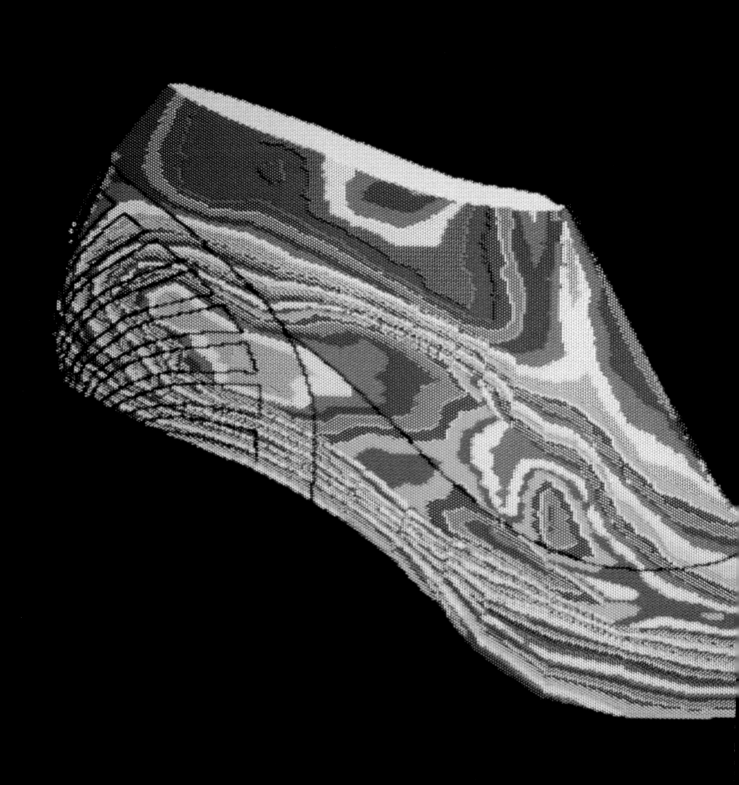

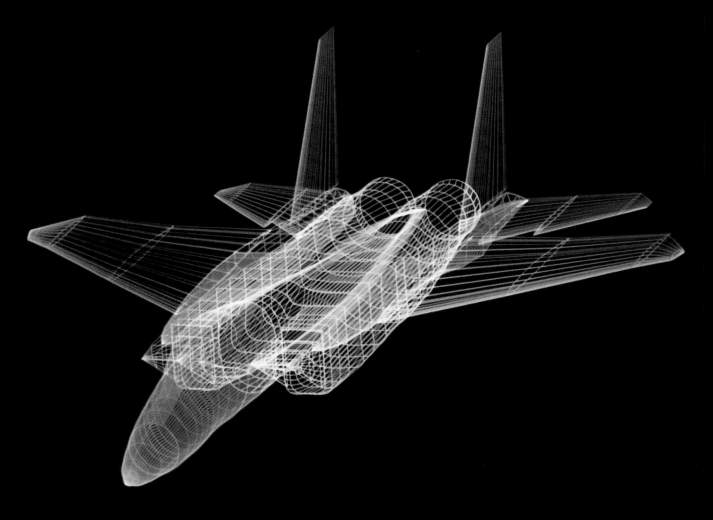

In this structūral view of the U.S.
Air Force's F-15 fighter, programmable colors delineate the plane's
five main assemblies: radar *(pink)*,
fuselage *(blue)*, wings *(yellow)*,
engines *(green)* and tail *(red)*.

Design Aids for
Foot and Flight

Computer-aided design lets shoe-
makers experiment with shapes and
textures on new styles like the
boot at left; software that generates
highlights and shadings produces
three-dimensional models of the traditional cobbler's last.

Re-creating a Mummy's Face

The face of a 3,400-year-old Egyptian mummy was reconstructed by Japanese researchers with software like that used by plastic surgeons. Data from a computerized X-ray scan *(below)* helped the computer to generate a structural model of the head *(bottom)* and then a lifelike image *(right)*.

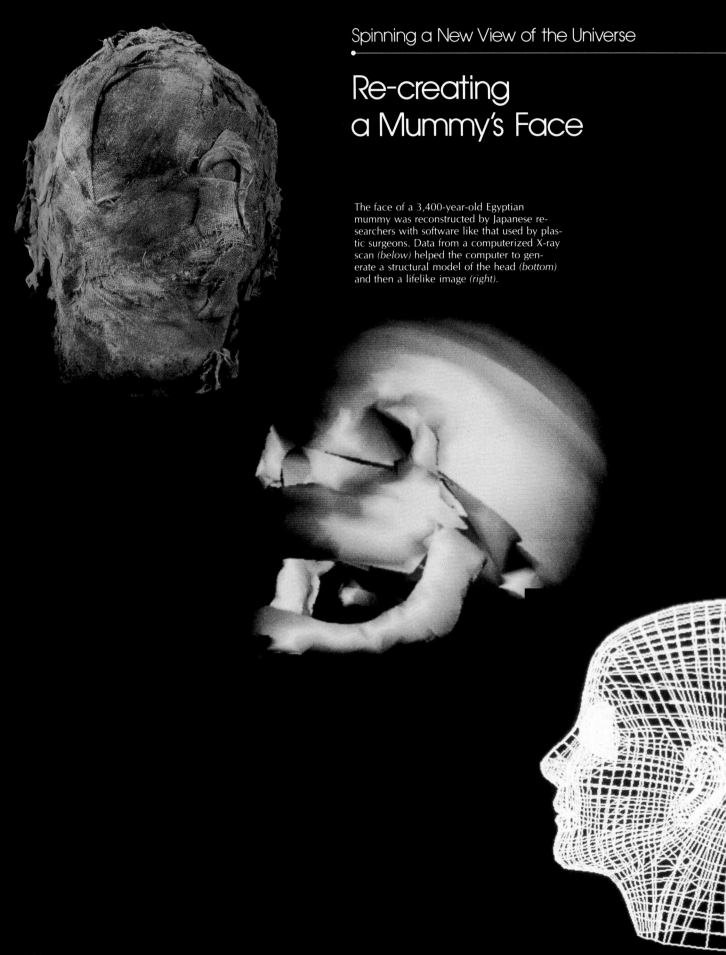

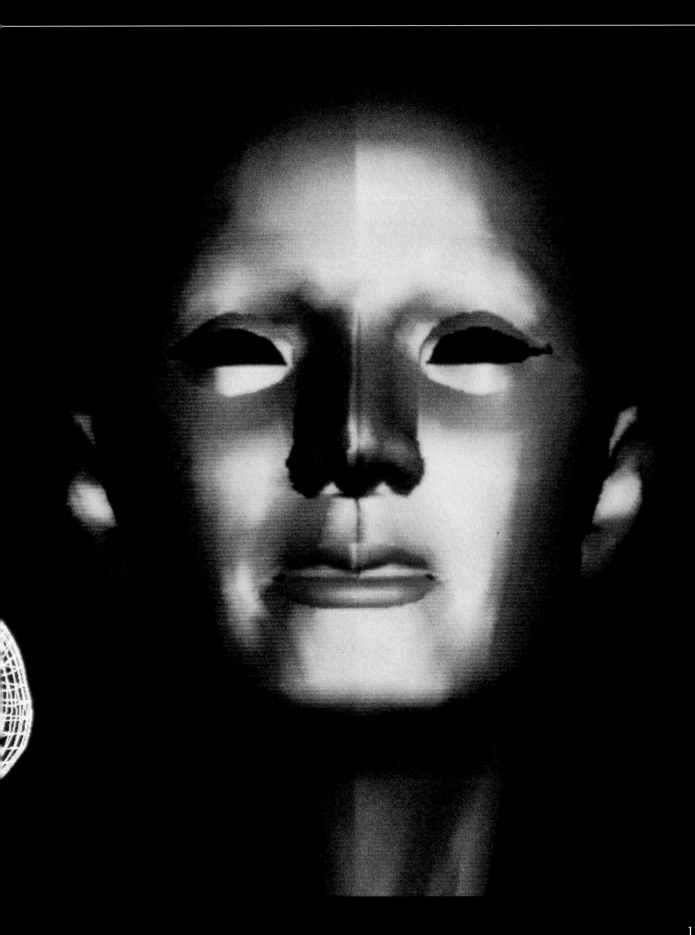

5

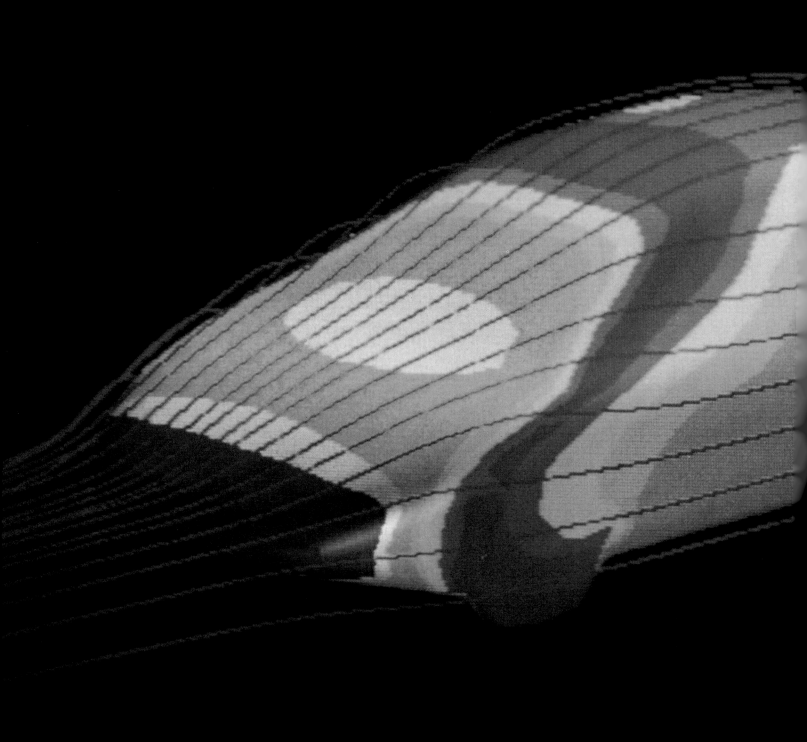

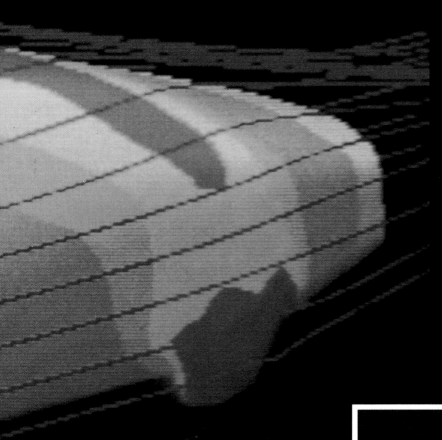

A simulated test of air flow on an experimental automobile reveals areas of high and low pressure; simulations can also be used to determine the precise effects of collisions.

This sequence of stick figures — extrapolated from high-speed film of a real pole vaulter's performance — permits a coach to analyze such flaws in technique as poor alignment at takeoff.

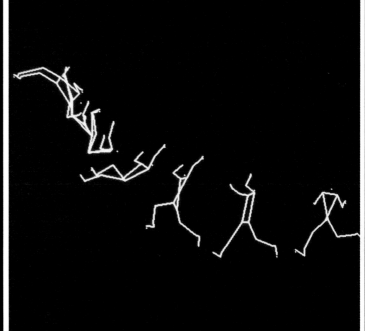

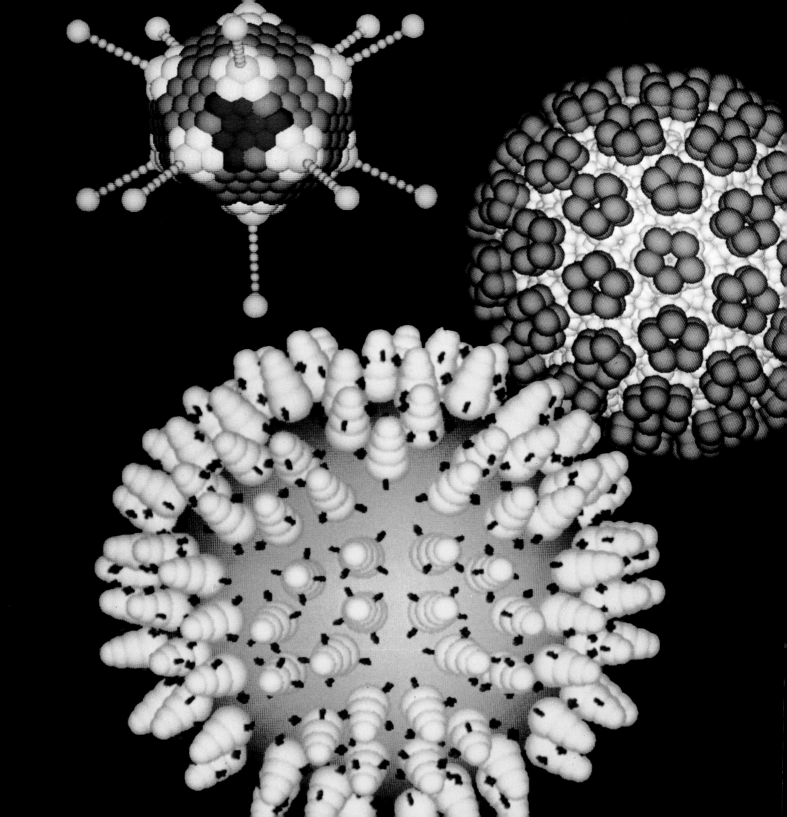

Computer models reveal the structures of microorganisms. Shown on the opposite page *(clockwise from top)* are: adenovirus, which causes colds in children; polyoma virus, which attacks mice; and Semliki Forest virus, which is carried by mosquitoes. Below, yellow amino acid chains coil within a tomato virus from which half of the exterior has been removed.

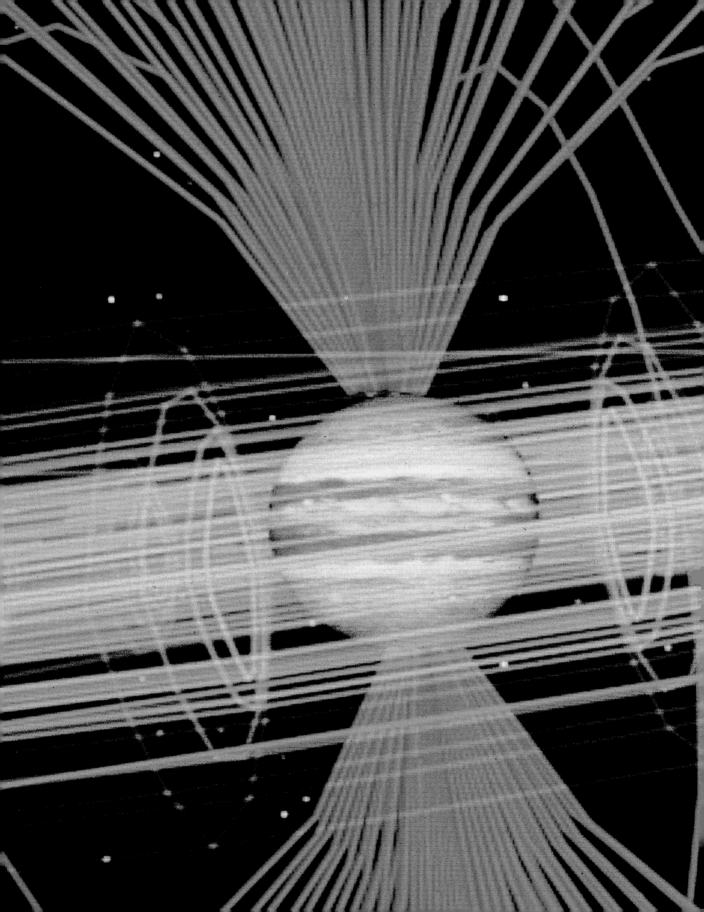

A computer model from an educational film shows a sodium cloud *(yellow)* and the path of one proton *(red)* within Jupiter's magnetic field *(blue)*.

Bibliography

Books

Barnes, Henry A., *The Man with the Red and Green Eyes*. New York: E. P. Dutton, 1965.

Brand, Stewart, ed., *Whole Earth Software Catalog*. Garden City, N.Y.: Quantum Press/Doubleday, 1984.

Curran, Susan, and Ray Curnow, *Overcoming Computer Illiteracy*. New York: Penguin Books, 1983.

Davies, William S., *Basic: Getting Started*. Reading, Mass.: Addison-Wesley, 1981.

Drury, Donald William, *The Art of Computer Programming*. Blue Ridge Summit, Pa.: Tab Books, 1983.

Eames, Charles, and Ray Eames, *A Computer Perspective*. Cambridge, Mass.: Harvard University Press, 1973.

Editors of Osborne/McGraw Hill, *The Osborne/McGraw Hill Home Computer Software Guide*. Berkeley, Calif.: Osborne/McGraw-Hill, 1984.

Evans, Christopher, *The Micro Millennium*. New York: Washington Square Press, 1979.

Fishman, Katharine Davis, *The Computer Establishment*. New York: Harper & Row, 1981.

Fox, Annie, and David Fox, *Armchair Basic: An Absolute Beginner's Guide to Programming in BASIC*. Berkeley, Calif.: Osborne/McGraw-Hill, 1983.

Freiberger, Paul, and Michael Swaine, *Fire in the Valley*. Berkeley, Calif.: Osborne/McGraw-Hill, 1984.

Gilbert, Glen A., *Air Traffic Control: The Uncrowded Sky*. Washington, D.C.: Smithsonian Institution Press, 1973.

Godman, Arthur, *The Color-Coded Guide to Microcomputers*. New York: Barnes & Noble Books, 1983.

Goldstine, Herman H., *The Computer from Pascal to von Neumann*. Princeton: Princeton University Press, 1972.

Hansen, Dirk, *The New Alchemists*. Boston: Little, Brown, 1982.

Helms, Harry, ed., *The McGraw-Hill Computer Handbook*. New York: McGraw-Hill, 1983.

Helms, Harry L., *Computer Language Reference Guide*. Indianapolis, Ind.: Howard W. Sams, 1980.

Horenstein, Henry, *ComputerWise*. New York: Random House, 1983.

Lafferty, Peter, *An Introduction to Computing*. New York: Simon & Schuster, 1983.

Laurie, Peter, *The Joy of Computers*. London: Hutchinson, 1983.

Levering, Robert, Michael Katz and Milton Moskowitz, *The Computer Entrepreneurs*. New York: New American Library, 1984.

Levy, Steven, *Hackers: Heroes of the Computer Revolution*. New York: Doubleday, 1984.

Metropolis, N., J. Howlett and Gian-Carlo Rota, eds., *A History of Computing in the Twentieth Century: A Collection of Essays*. New York: Academic Press, 1980.

Moreau, René, *The Computer Comes of Age*. Cambridge, Mass.: The M.I.T. Press, 1984.

Nash, Edward L., *Direct Marketing: Strategy/Planning/Execution*. New York: McGraw-Hill, 1982.

Poole, Lon, Martin McNiff and Steven Cook, *Your Atari Computer*. Berkeley, Calif., Osborne/McGraw-Hill, 1982.

Ralston, Anthony, and Edwin D. Reilly Jr., eds., *Encyclopedia of Computer Science and Engineering*. New York: Van Nostrand Reinhold, 1983.

Richman, Ellen, *The Random House Book of Computer Literacy*. New York: Vintage Books, 1983.

Rodwell, Peter, *The Personal Computer Handbook*. New York: Barron's, 1983.

Sammet, Jean E., *Programming Languages: History and Fundamentals*. Englewood Cliffs, N.J.: Prentice-Hall, 1969.

Sanders, Donald H., *Computers Today*. New York: McGraw-Hill, 1983.

Wexelblat, Richard L., ed., *History of Programming Languages*. New York: Academic Press, 1981.

Periodicals

Brand, Stewart, ed., "Keep Designing." *Whole Earth Review*, May 1985.

Browne, Malcolm, "Ultimate Video Game." *Discover*, August 1983.

Brownlee, Shannon, "Weather Forecasting — How Exact Is It?" *Discover*, April 1985.

"Computer Software." *Scientific American*, September 1984.

d'Ambrosio, Bruce, "Expert Systems — Myth or Reality?" *BYTE*, January 1985.

Duda, Richard O., "Expert Systems Research." *Science*, April 15, 1983.

Eskow, Dennis, "PM 'Flies' the Shuttle Simulator." *Popular Mechanics*, November 1982.

Fluegelman, Andrew, "In Quest of True BASIC." *PC World*, November 1984.

Gardner, Martin:
"Computer as Scientist." *Discover*, June 1983.
"Traveling Salesman's Travail." *Discover*, April 1985.

Gifford, David, and Alfred Spector, "The TWA Reservation System." *Communications of the ACM*, July 1984.

Gleick, James, "They're Getting Better about Predicting the Weather." *The New York Times Magazine*, January 27, 1985.

Immel, A. Richard, "Electric Pencil's Rise and Fall." *Popular Computing*, August 1984.

Knight, John R., "A Case Study: Airlines Reservations Systems." *Proceedings of the IEEE*, November 1972.

"The Mechanization of Work." *Scientific American*, September 1982.

Nulty, Peter, "The Bar-Coding of America," *Fortune*, December 27, 1982.

Olson, Steve:
"Pathways of Choice," *Mosaic*, July/August 1983.
"Sage of Software," *Science 84*, January/February 1984.

"$100,000 'Brain' Keeps Denver Traffic Rolling." *Popular Science*, January 1953.

Popular Computing, "Special Report: Computer Languages." September 1983.

Roberts, H. Edward, and William Yates:
"Altair 8800." *Popular Electronics*, January 1975.
"Build the Altair 800." *Popular Electronics*, February 1975.

Rose, Frank, "Black Knight of AI." *Science 85*, March 1985.

Savani, Jacquelyn, "Supercomputing Arrives." *Princeton Weekly Bulletin*, March 4, 1985.

Shell, Ellen Ruppel, "The Brain behind BASIC." *Technology Illustrated*, December/January 1983.

Smith, Lloyd, and Kent Madsen, "Nonstop Transaction Processing." *Datamation*, March 1983.

Taubes, Gary, "Mathematics of Chaos." *Discover,* September 1984.
Taylor, Alexander L., III, "The Wizard inside the Machines." *Time,* April 16, 1984.
Tesler, Lawrence, "Programming Languages." *Scientific American,* September 1984.
Toong, Hoo-min D., and Amar Gupta, "Personal Computers." *Scientific American,* December 1982.
"TX-0: Its Past and Present," *Computer Museum Report,* Spring 1984.

Waldrop, M. Mitchell:
"Computer Vision." *Science,* June 15, 1984.
"Machinations of Thought," *Science 85,* March 1985.
"The Necessity of Knowledge," *Science,* March 23, 1984.
Other Publications
The Home Computer Course. London: Orbis Publications, 1984.
Money Guide: Personal Computers. Time Inc., 1984.
U.S. Department of Commerce, *A Competitive Assessment of the U.S. Software Industry.* Washington, D.C.: U.S. Government Printing Office, 1984.

Acknowledgments

The index for this book was prepared by Mel Ingber. The editors also are indebted to the following: **In Great Britain:** Berkshire, Reading—Austin Woods, European Centre for Medium Range Weather Forecasts. **In the United States:** California—El Segundo: James Furlong, Computer Sciences Corporation; Los Angeles: S. E. Rowe, Los Angeles Department of Transportation; Pasadena: Sylvie J. Rueff, JPL Computer Graphics Lab, California Institute of Technology; San Francisco: Rick Beebe, Russell Fenwick and Marcus Gonzalez, Bank of America; San Rafael: Jennifer Godward, Micropro International Corp.; Sunnyvale: Troy Cumpton and David Zempel, Lockheed; Colorado—Denver: Edward Cleary, Leigh, Scott and Cleary; Maryland—Baltimore: Jack Redel, Marketing Direct, Inc.; Silver Spring: Donald E. Witten, National Weather Service; Massachusetts—Concord: Stephen A. Kallis Jr., Digital Equipment Corporation; Minnesota—Mendota Heights: Dennis E. Whitt, TeleSciences Inc.; New York —Schenectady: Richard Murray, Union College; North Carolina —Charlotte: Joseph Siwiec, IBM; Ohio—Dayton: John O'Gorman, National Cash Register; Pennsylvania—Philadelphia: Dr. Herman H. Goldstine, American Philosophical Society; Texas—Dallas-Fort Worth: Karen Cooke, American Airlines; Virginia—Alexandria: Jack Kay, JHK & Associates, and Leo Toralballa, Time-Life Books Inc.; Washington, D.C.: David Whiteford, Transportation Research Board, National Research Council.

Picture Credits

The sources for the illustrations that appear in this book are listed below. Credits from left to right are separated by semicolons; from top to bottom by dashes.
Cover, 6, 7: Art by Matt McMullen. 8: UPI/Bettmann Newsphotos. 10: Courtesy The Science Museum, London; courtesy The National Portrait Gallery, London — Derek Bayes, courtesy The Science Museum, London. 11: Culver Pictures. 12, 13: Wolf/SEMANA Publicada; Larry Sherer, courtesy Library of Congress. 15: King's College Library, Cambridge University. 17: Wide World; Department of the Navy. 19: Art by Matt McMullen. 20, 21: Art by Matt McMullen(3); David W. Zempel and Troy Cumpton at Lockheed Missiles and Space Company in Sunnyvale, California. 22, 23: Art by Matt McMullen. 24, 33-55: Art by Jeffrey Smith. 56, 57: © Robert Langridge/U.C.S.F./Rainbow; created by artist Damon Rarey on an Aurora/100 Videographics System for Varian Associates, Inc., 1981 — © Dan McCoy/Rainbow; McDonnell Douglas Corporation — James A. Sugar/Black Star — Dr. James F. Blinn/Computer Graphics Lab/JPL; generated at GMAC using ISSCO software. 59, 60: The M.I.T. Museum. 63: © 1984 Forrest M. Mims III. 64: Art by Frederic F. Bigio from B-C Graphics. 65: Art by Frederic F. Bigio from B-C Graphics — Computer program, courtesy of Osborne/McGraw-Hill from *Your Atari Computer* © 1982 by Lon Poole, Martin McNiff and Steven Cook. 66, 67: Art by Matt McMullen, computer screens by Circuit Studio. 68: Courtesy Lee Felsenstein. 70, 71: Doug Wilson; Margaret Kern Wozniak — Michael Alexander; Rick Browne; Paul Hirschberger; Wayne C. Kodey/*Time,* art by Matt McMullen. 72: Ashton-Tate(2) — Simpson Kalisher for *Fortune*(2); Richard Howard, art by Matt McMullen. 74: Paul Lutus. 75-81: Art by Matt McMullen. 82, 83: Airbrush illustration by Matt McMullen, line art by Frederic F. Bigio from B-C Graphics, computer screens by Teresa M. Nussbaumer/Circuit Studio. 84, 85: Art by Mike Newman, DICOMED Corporation. 91-98: Art by Tyrone Huntley. 99: Art by Tyrone Huntley, computer screens by JHK and Associates. 100: Hitachi, Ltd., Tokyo. 102: Dr. Martin S. Burkhead; Los Alamos National Laboratory and Dr. Martin S. Burkhead. 104, 105: John Bowden/ © 1985 *Discover.* 107: Evans & Sutherland Computer Corporation. 110: Dan McCoy/Rainbow. 113: Arthur Olson, Scripps Clinic and Nelson Max, Lawrence Livermore National Laboratory. 114, 115: Jerry Mason/Photo Researchers; Evans & Sutherland Computer Corporation. 116, 117: K. Kurita/Gamma-Liaison. 118, 119: © Hank Morgan/Rainbow; John Morgan. 120, 121: Robert Feldmann/NIH, copied by Dan McCoy/Rainbow (3); Arthur Olson, Scripps Clinic and Nelson Max, Livermore National Laboratory. 122, 123: Dr. James F. Blinn/Computer Graphics Lab/JPL.

Index

Time-Life Books Inc.
is a wholly owned subsidiary of
THE TIME INC. BOOK COMPANY

President and Chief Executive Officer: Kelso F. Sutton
President, Time Inc. Books Direct:
Christopher T. Linen

TIME-LIFE BOOKS INC.

EDITOR: George Constable
Executive Editor: Ellen Phillips
Director of Design: Louis Klein
Director of Editorial Resources: Phyllis K. Wise
Director of Photography and Research:
John Conrad Weiser

PRESIDENT: John M. Fahey Jr.
Senior Vice Presidents: Robert M. DeSena,
Paul R. Stewart, Curtis G. Viebranz, Joseph J. Ward
Vice Presidents: Stephen L. Bair, Bonita L.
Boezeman, Mary P. Donohoe, Stephen L. Goldstein,
Juanita T. James, Andrew P. Kaplan, Trevor Lunn,
Susan J. Maruyama, Robert H. Smith
New Product Development: Yuri Okuda,
Donia Ann Steele
Supervisor of Quality Control: James King

PUBLISHER: Joseph J. Ward

Editorial Operations
Copy Chief: Diane Ullius
Production: Celia Beattie
Library: Louise D. Forstall

Computer Composition: Gordon E. Buck (Manager),
Deborah G. Tait, Monika D. Thayer,
Janet Barnes Syring, Lillian Daniels

Correspondents: Elisabeth Kraemer-Singh (Bonn);
Christina Lieberman (New York); Maria Vincenza
Aloisi (Paris); Ann Natanson (Rome). Valuable
assistance was also provided by: Nihal Tamraz
(Cairo); Millicent Trowbridge, Christine Hinze
(London); Carolyn Chubet (New York); Dick Berry
(Tokyo).

Library of Congress Cataloging in Publication Data

Software.
  (Understanding computers)
  Includes bibliographical references.
  1. Computer software.   I. Time-Life Books.   II. Series.
QA76.754.S64 1990   005—dc20   89-39522
ISBN 0-8094-7554-5
ISBN 0-8094-7555-3 (lib. bdg.)

For information on and a full description of any Time-Life
Books series listed, please call 1-800-621-7026 or write:
Reader Information
Time-Life Customer Service
P.O. Box C-32068
Richmond, Virginia 23261-2068

Time-Life Books Inc. offers a wide range of fine recordings,
including a *Rock 'n' Roll Era* series. For subscription
information, call 1-800-621-7026 or write Time-Life Music,
P.O. Box C-32068, Richmond, Virginia 23261-2068.

UNDERSTANDING COMPUTERS

SERIES DIRECTOR: Roberta Conlan

Editorial Staff for *Software*
Designer: Ellen Robling
Associate Editor: Neil Kagan (pictures)
Series Administrator: Rita Thievon Mullin
Researchers:
Susan S. Blair
Esther Ferington
Elise Ritter Gibson
Norma E. Kennedy
Sara Mark
Text Editors:
Russell B. Adams Jr.
Peter Pocock
Assistant Designer: Robert K. Herndon
Copy Coordinator: Anthony K. Pordes
Picture Coordinator: Renée DeSandies
Editorial Assistant: Diana L. Sims

Special Contributors: Ronald H. Bailey, Sarah Brash,
Richard Immel, John I. Merritt, Charles C. Smith (text);
Ann Corson (research)

GENERAL CONSULTANT

ISABEL LIDA NIRENBERG has dealt with a wide range of
computer applications, from the analysis of data collected by the Pioneer space probes to the matching of children and families for adoption agencies. She works at the
Computer Center at the State University of New York at
Albany, and assists faculty and students there with microcomputer applications.

OTHER CONSULTANTS

GWEN BELL is the President of The Computer Museum
in Boston, Massachusetts.

J. KIRK DEMAREE is President of Computer Tutors, a
company that provides consulting and instruction on microcomputers in Alexandria, Virginia.

JOHN R. KNIGHT, a Senior Engineer for IBM Corporation, was for 12 years involved in the development of
computerized airline reservations systems that currently
serve the commercial air industry.

UTA C. MERZBACH has served as the Curator of the
mathematical and computing collections of the Smithsonian Institution's National Museum of American History since 1963.

R. BRUCE MORRIN is an Associate Professor at Embry-
Riddle Aeronautical University in Daytona Beach, Florida, where he directs the Air Traffic Control program.

MICHAEL WISE is a Program Designer and Technical
Consultant for Broderbund Software in San Rafael, California, where he develops video games and personal
productivity software.

REVISIONS STAFF

EDITOR: Lee Hassig

Writer: Esther Ferington
Assistant Designer: Tina Taylor
Copy Coordinator: Anne Farr
Picture Coordinator: Katherine Griffin

Consultant: Michael R. Williams, a professor of
computer science at the University of Calgary in
Canada, is the author of *A History of Computing
Technology.*